ON THE
CURRY
TRAIL

ON THE CURRY TRAIL

Chasing the Flavor That
Seduced the World

— IN 50 RECIPES —

RAGHAVAN IYER

WORKMAN PUBLISHING
NEW YORK

Library of Congress Cataloging-in-Publication Data is available.
ISBN 978-1-5235-1121-1

Design by Rae Ann Spitzenberger and Sarah Smith
Cover design by Becky Terhune
Cover illustration by Anisa Makhoul
Illustrations by Neethi (Asia),
Anisa Makhoul (Africa & The Middle East), Jenny Bowers (Europe & Oceania),
and Marisol Ortega (The Americas)

Workman books are available at special discounts when purchased in bulk for
premiums and sales promotions as well as for fundraising or educational use.
Special editions or book excerpts can also be created to specification.
For details, please contact specialmarkets@hbgusa.com.

Workman Publishing Co., Inc.,
a subsidiary of Hachette Book Group, Inc.
1290 Avenue of the Americas
New York, NY 10104
workman.com

WORKMAN is a registered trademark of Workman Publishing Co., Inc.,
a subsidiary of Hachette Book Group, Inc.

Printed in South Korea on responsibly sourced paper.
First printing January 2023

10 9 8 7 6 5 4 3 2 1

**TO MY PARTNER
OF MORE THAN
THIRTY-EIGHT YEARS,
TERRY ERICKSON.**

*You have been a steadfast presence in my life
through sickness and in health and without you,
this book could never have been penned.*

CONTENTS

INTRODUCTION

INDIA AND BEYOND

In 2008, I authored a book called *660 Curries* that captured the essence of a curry as seen through the eyes of cooks and their eaters within the Indian subcontinent (including Pakistan, Sri Lanka, and Nepal). These saucy dishes anchored their position at the table, at every meal, evidence of their existence dating back to India (and Pakistan) around 4000 BCE, along the Indus River, and flourishing with the sophisticated Indus civilization of Mohenjo-Daro and Harappa between 2500 and 1600 BCE. Mortars and pestles pounded spices like saffron, sesame seeds, mustard seeds, cumin, tamarind, turmeric, ginger, garlic, and peppercorns, flavoring dishes that included meats, fish, wild game, barley, wheat, rice, peas, lentils, chickpeas, and even fruits like pomegranate, dates, and bananas.

> "If any dish deserves to be called global, it is curry. From Newfoundland to the Antarctic, from Beijing to Warsaw, there is scarcely a place where curries are not enjoyed."
>
> —COLLEEN TAYLOR SEN, *CURRY: A GLOBAL HISTORY*

The sophistication of Indian cuisine, balancing six taste elements of hot, sour, sweet, bitter, salty, and astringent (umami was a much later discovery), is deeply embedded in the annals of ayurvedic medicine, from around the first century BCE, a science that dictated the role of spices, herbs, and other flavorings to regulate various body types for a sense of equilibrium. Temperature contrasts, colors, aromas, and textures were under consideration as well, as practitioners of ayurveda combined seemingly disparate ingredients with highly nuanced results, balancing the therapeutic qualities inherent in food. Every dish had a specific spicing technique, every stew and sauce a particular name. The word *curry* was nonexistent in any of the languages spoken in India for thousands of years until the British set deep colonial roots in this subcontinent.

This book, *The Curry Trail*, follows the journey and the influence of the colonials and the Indian diaspora itself to comprehend the introduction and acceptance of curries, in all their forms, including curry powders and pastes, around the globe. To understand the presence of the British and the subsequent concept of curry powders, it is best to follow

First we had Mulligatawny soup,

Which made us all perspire,

For the cook, that obstinate nincompoop,

Had flavoured it hot as fire.

Next a tremendous fragmentary dish

Of salmon was carried in,—

The taste was rather of oil than fish,

With a palpable touch of tin.

Then, when the salmon was swept away,

We'd a duckey stew, with peas,

And the principal feature of that entree,

Was its circumambient grease.

Then came the pride of my small farm-yard,—

A magnificent Michaelmas goose:

Heavens! his breast was a trifle hard;

As for his leg, the deuce!

Last, we'd a curry of ancient fowl:

In terror a portion I took,—

Hot?—I could hardly suppress a how—

Curse that fiend of a cook.

—**"The Police-Wallah's Little Dinner," 1871**

the spice trail (and particularly the path of the peppercorn) to and from India. India's geographic location has long placed it at the crossroads of international trade routes, and the spices, which for many years grew only on its land and that of its neighbors, made India more than just a convenient stopping point. They made it a destination.

Even though spices and other goods were being traded via land routes during the Neolithic period (which began around 10,000 BCE), it is the emergence of viable sea routes that catapulted the spice business from the East to the European West (spanning almost 10,000 miles) and forged a conduit for the maritime silk route. The Austronesians (those cultures and countries comprising people speaking Austronesian languages from Taiwan, Madagascar, Oceania, and the seafaring parts of Southeast Asia) were early builders of oceangoing ships and established maritime spice routes that included southern India and Ceylon (now Sri Lanka) as early as 1500 BCE, eventually reaching Africa and the Arabian Peninsula. Indians were already trading peppercorns with the Middle East (by land) around 2000 BCE; they experienced a boom in the spice trade with the Arabs and Phoenicians 800 years later when the rulers from East India controlled cloves and cinnamon from Sri Lanka and the Moluccas (now Indonesia).

BLACK GOLD BECKONS

The native *Piper nigrum* vine wrapped around other plants, usually coffee. Its green fruit, when poached in boiling water and dried in the sun, shriveled to become what we know as black peppercorns, bursting with the seduction of a slow burn on the tongue. That's what took traders, rulers, warriors, marauders, preachers, and refugees to southwestern India off the coast of Malabar (now called Kerala) in droves starting around 500 BCE to procure massive amounts of this beguiling spice, which was often referred to as black gold. Indian traders were supplying ginger, black pepper, cardamom, and cinnamon to the Romans via the Arabs until the Romans, by the first century BCE, figured out a way to cut out the middleman and get to India by ship to procure spices directly, using the flow of monsoon winds across the Indian Ocean.

Even though the Arab traders, for many years, were considered to be the controllers of the spice trade between Asia and Europe, it wasn't until the Europeans established transatlantic and transpacific trade routes that the supply chain control transferred to the Europeans, truly shaping the Western world's economies. The first Islamic rulers in India were the Mughals, or Mongols (descendants of Genghis Khan), who arrived and spread their power from 1526 CE to 1857 CE. The period was rich and vibrant with culture, architecture, and cuisine (saffron, nuts, dried fruits, black pepper, cardamom,

A FRAGRANT JOURNEY

Curry has crisscrossed the globe, setting roots in kitchens from Australia to Antarctica. Yes, you read that correctly. There may be no recipe for penguin curry in this book—thankfully, since penguins are protected—but there is evidence suggesting curries made their way onto the menu for members of certain expeditions as early as 1902.

34

35

36

37

38

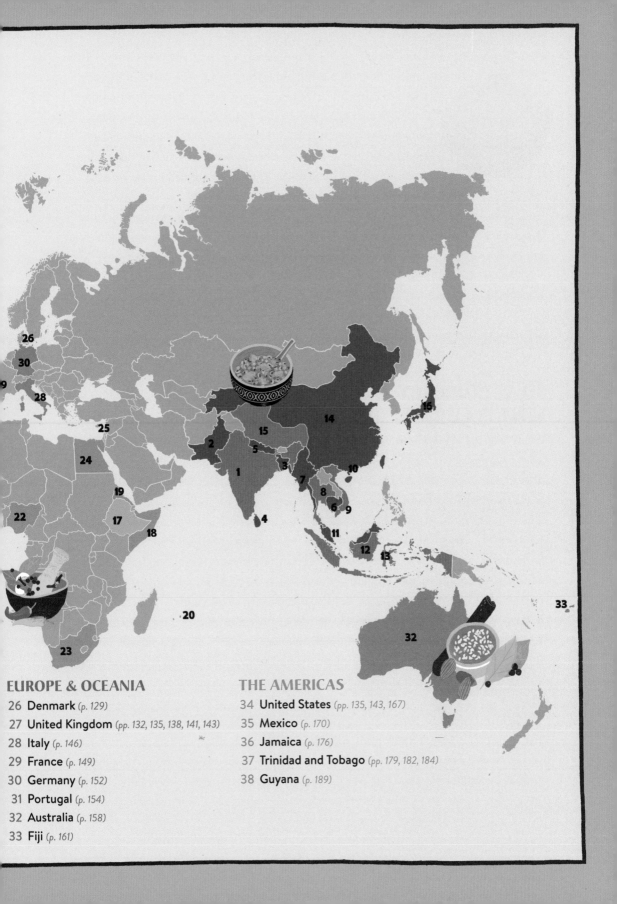

cinnamon, and other aromatics). The British, who had come in as traders and, in 1600, formed the East India Company, soon became a commercial superpower. Eventually the British government supplanted the East India Company and gained control of the country in 1857 under a system known as the British Raj, taking formal control of India as the Mughals crumbled under growing religious strife with non-Muslims.

The Europeans took control over other parts of India as well—the Dutch and the Danes spreading their influence between 1605 and 1869; the French between 1668 and 1954; and the Portuguese between 1505 and 1961. But it was under the British Raj, which lasted until 1947, that Indian stews and saucy dishes were bastardized into monochromatic Anglo-Indian cuisine. This muted the vibrant complexity of Indian foods—dishes traditionally layered with spices and sauces and cooked in a multitude of ways—to a duller panacea blend that appealed to the regimented senses of the British.

SO, IS CURRY BY ANOTHER NAME STILL A CURRY?

Simply put, the answer is an unequivocal yes. We know that the idea of curries—saucy, brothy, gravy-rich, and stewy dishes, from simple to complex, made with spices, spice blends, herbs, and nuts—has thrived in the Indian subcontinent for at least 6,000 years. The renowned historian and writer K. T. Achaya, in his indispensible work of biblical proportions, *Indian Food: A Historical Companion*, attributes any spiced dish from the south as a *kari* (a Tamil word), which was called a *caril* as early as 1502 CE by the Portuguese. Alan Davidson, author of *The Oxford Companion to Food*, concurs with curry being derived from kari, and explains its association with the soupy dishes of South India that are spiced with a roasted medley of coriander, cumin, curry (kari) leaves, mustard seeds, black pepper, fenugreek, turmeric, cinnamon, cloves, and cardamom. Here's another interesting explanation, however, this one from author Dharam Jit Singh, who wrote *Classic Cooking from India*: "Curry is a word that comes from the Hindustani *turcarri*. In the colloquial it is shortened to *turri*, which in Anglo-Saxon usage is called curry."

The British took the names of many of these individual dishes—like kormas with saffron and nuts, potent onion-soused dopiazas, and heady black cardamom–scented and cockscomb-colored roghan josh—and grouped them in one swooping word: *curry*. It was a catchall for any dish that was Indian. They had their bawarchis (cooks) combine a specific array of spices and pound them into a more submissive mélange they called curry powder—mellow in heat, and scented with the spices they traded across the world and their colonies to benefit the king's or queen's treasure chest. They instructed their cooks to anglicize the curries, fashioning rich roux-style sauces that swathed their meats, fish, poultry, and vegetables—all topped with sweet-tart apples, sugary mango chutney, desiccated coconut shreds, and sultanas (golden raisins). Not surprisingly, this style of cooking never appealed to the Indians, who preferred the nuances of the dishes they made in their own home kitchens. These highly individualized creations used the age-old teachings to harmonize the elements of taste, color, texture, temperature, and aroma—the subtleties (and, often, laboriousness) of which were not appreciated by the British.

Hannah Glasse's recipe "To make a curry the Indian Way," published in 1747 in her book *The Art of Cookery Made Plain and Easy*, was the first curry recipe published in English. It set the benchmark for the British to blend and carry curry powders back to their birth country, to relive their experiences with Anglo-Indian curries. This was further cemented with a "stock receipt for curry powder" from Colonel A. R. Kenney-Herbert in 1885, listing must-have spices like turmeric, ground coriander seeds, cumin seeds, fenugreek seeds, mustard seeds, dried red chilies, black peppercorns, poppy seeds, and dried ginger. *Law's Grocer's Manual*, first published in London in the late 1800s, dictated twelve to nineteen ingredients in commercial curry powders, including rice and tapioca flour.

HOW DID CURRY CULTURE TRAVEL?

The myriad traders, conquerors, refugees, and colonizers, upon return to their birthlands, assimilated spices and techniques that shaped the world of curries into their existing meal patterns. Many of the British expats, after their stint serving the Raj in India, managed to take their ayahs (servants) and bawarchis to Britain, making sure their penchant for their Anglo-Indian mulligatawny (see page 139) and other anglicized curries was assuaged on a regular basis. But most significantly, when Indians left their country to travel, emigrate, work, or study in many of the nations that had colonized them, their food and curry culture were steadfast companions on their journey, spreading the gospel of curries, albeit with the convenience of curry powders and pastes. Writer Colleen Taylor Sen hit the nail on the head when she wrote in *Curry: A Global History* that "while the British brought curry to their English-speaking colonies, it was

Indians themselves who took their eating habits to the rest of the empire."

One example is the Bangladeshis (previously called Sylhetis), who were and are major players in the British culinary scene. They worked the engine rooms of British steamboats in the mid-nineteenth century. Once they realized that the wages being paid to them were a fifth of what a Caucasian garnered, many jumped ship and settled in ports from Rangoon (now Yangon) to Singapore to Southampton, and to New York. One well-known Sylheti, a Mr. Ali, opened a small coffee shop in the early 1900s, in East London's Canning Town, serving rice and curry to many of the boatmen. Soon a trend was established, as many followed suit with cafés on Sandys Row, Brick Lane, and Commercial Road. Once the British immigration laws changed in the late 1950s, Sylhetis were able to bring in families and relatives from "back home," who helped them run these cafés that served the foods they and their clientele yearned for, flavors that satiated their nostalgic palates.

Writer Cecilia Leong-Salobir, in her book *Food Culture in Colonial Asia: A Taste of Empire*, shared sociologist Priscilla Parkhurst Ferguson's description of the moment when we start referring to a community's or culture's food as a cuisine: "Culinary preparations become a cuisine when, and only when, the preparations are articulated and formalized, and enter the public domain." And this is what happened with the British rendition of Indian curries. It created an awareness among British people at home and in British colonies across the globe.

Eurasian Curries

The various empires that swept across landscapes and communities, expanding and contracting, were a very significant force by which food culture traveled and evolved. Looking at the dishes of empires dating from 1000 BCE to 600 CE, every one of them had sauces that were either reminiscent of or strong examples of "curries" (I've added quotes because the word was not known by its English name until years later). Many of the Eurasian empires that touched, encompassed, or traded with India were significant in the creation of "curry" cultures in many other countries.

Food preparation techniques, ingredients, and combinations traveled across and were consumed by neighboring empires. Within a single empire, the controlling powers soaked in elements of regional cuisines and transferred foundations of the empire's food culture (pre-established, inherited, learned, and adapted) throughout their territory and beyond. Neighboring empires and countries were influenced by travelers, merchants, the tastes of the wealthy, and the migration of philosophies and ingredients. Furthermore, many empires passed their cuisine on to the empire that succeeded them or to the empires that coexisted with them. Often the empires were emulated for their power, one source of which was the empires' food. For example, the cuisine of the Persian empire was "co-opted" from Mesopotamian culinary customs, and the Mughal and Roman empires held on to the foods of the Persian empire. Nomadic people living on the Central Asian steppes took Roman ingredients and food techniques to China, and the Romans, like many empires before and after them, diffused their evolving cuisine and its ingredients across their territories: coriander, fennel, garlic, leeks, and mustard are just some of the many plants thought to have reached Britain through Roman propagation. As my colleague and friend Rachel Laudan said in her award-winning (rightfully so!) book, *Cuisine and Empire: Cooking in World History*, "by 200 CE, a chain of interlinked cuisines stretched from the Roman Empire in the West through the empires of Persia and northern India and across the steppes to the Han Empire in northern China."

In those early years, curry was developed (by internal and external influences) in India and was transferred out of India across various territories. But over hundreds and thousands of years the waves of cultural, political, and religious change muddled and muted some of those direct culinary lines, and as states, countries, and cuisines shifted, some of the curry dishes were transformed to the point where just a spice or an element of a sauce spoke to its memory. And then, many generations later, a new wave of change—for example, brought by a new branch of trade or a new governing body—swept over, setting a new group of curry dishes atop a cuisine that had already been shaped by curries a thousand years before. And it seems remarkable that that new curry so easily adapted to the cuisine, which already had, perhaps, a yogurt sauce and spiced rice prepared to meld with it. But in reality, the great-grandmother of curries was there all along, transformed into a dish or diffused into many fundamentals of a cuisine (such as cooking techniques, ingredients, flavor combinations) that were particular to that empire's history of cuisine or blend of culture.

European and Western Curries

Although the spices from India and the Spice Islands (Indonesian birthplace of nutmeg, mace, and cloves) were widely distributed in Europe by the end of the Middle Ages (the end of the fifteenth century), I haven't seen much indication that the culture of creating curries often traveled with the spices. Just because the spices and ingredients were available, it didn't mean that the knowledge and interest in preparing curries were transported as well. It seems like curry didn't start to travel until the communities who made it started to travel, in larger numbers than just the representative spice traders.

The documentation I've read so far shows that curry travels with the people who make it. For example, after the British spent time in India they carried the making of curry back to their home countries, supported its development in British colonies, and inspired its development in countries it traded with, like Japan. Significantly, curry made lasting impressions in countries where newly arrived Indians lived and worked. This happened, for example, when Indians left India for the Caribbean, Fiji, South Africa, and elsewhere under Britain's indentured labor policies (from 1838 to 1919, 1.5 million Indians left India and only one-third returned) and when Indian communities left India independently—such as those who emigrated to Israel and the Gujarati traders and businessmen who followed Indian rural laborers to Fiji and Africa. Racist immigration policies—the fluxion of open and closed borders, caps on numbers of immigrants, and restrictions on marriages, for example—significantly impacted the Indian community and food cultures of many countries, either thwarting or supporting burgeoning Indian cuisines.

Asian and Eastern Curries

This is a very long and complex history, which is blurred by shifting borders and the movement of people, empires, food, and trade over time. It's also blurred by a Western focus on cultural history and influence, skewing the perspective of some of the widely available articles and books on the topic of curry. In general, I've seen several predominant story lines. Food culture traveled with communities as they moved around or were forced to relocate. Enforced migrations—due to, for example, pre–Modern era expansion, climate change, and war—often resulted in one food culture either blending with or being obscured by another. Food culture also traveled with trade and micro-migration, of which the complexity of the sea networks of the Austronesians is just one example. According to writer and historian Jayanta Sengupta, "if one looks at the Indian Ocean, for example, in an area that includes coastal East Africa, the Red Sea, the Persian Gulf, the Indian subcontinent, and what is now Southeast Asia (and beyond the Indian Ocean regional, coastal China and Japan), one finds a long history of connection. These connections probably reached their zenith from the twelfth century onward, and especially during the century between the latter

half of the thirteenth century and first half of the fourteenth (i.e., from 1250 to 1350). During this time, long-distance trade over land, but especially over sea, had resulted in a truly spectacular set of economic relations and cultural encounters. Economies around the world connected by these routes boomed, as did new forms of cultural expression."

In terms of India's influence on eastern curries, I see a very layered and long history of cross-cultural influence. Part of the sway is from being neighbors, and the trade and literal cross-pollination that happens from being in close proximity. The migration of people from India to live in other countries (such as Sri Lanka and Burma) is significant, and its impact has been documented for thousands of years. Religious food culture from India—for example, the Buddhist and Hindu practices of setting the table with rice—influenced many countries in Asia. I have managed to peel off an onion layer to reveal how ancient Indian empires propelled the transmission of curry culture, tracking the culinary changes as India's territory, and therefore influence, expanded and contracted over time. One line of inquiry is pretty direct: to follow the spices that were transported from India into some of these countries (chilies and coriander, for example, were introduced to Thailand). In some of these cases, the receiving countries were already making stew-like dishes (curries) with fresh herbs, but spices from India influenced their cooking, forming new types of curries; and in a few cases, Indian residents in these countries became known for introducing a specific dish (aromatic duck curry in Thailand, for example).

Middle Eastern Curries

This feels like a story of trade, empire, religion, migration, and admiration—what a great engaging book or movie is all about! Arabs had some of the earliest wide-reaching trade networks. And the Islamic and Persian empires controlled significant eras and areas of cultural and material trade, spreading from North Africa across the Middle East and India and into Southeast Asia. I have the impression that curries traveled across the Middle East through periods of empires and Islam expanding east and west, and the Middle East (being in the middle, and being a part of the wide-reaching networks) developed a cuisine based on the best ingredients and techniques it was exposed to. Western/Christian rulers admired Islamic and Persian cuisine, spices, and aristocratic culture and, in emulation, they imported spices and re-created dishes of the Middle East.

In a more direct sense, a specifically Indian cuisine has a strong presence in some Middle Eastern countries due to shared rulers and shifting borders. These days, as Colleen Taylor Sen observed in her book *Curry: A Global History*, "curries and Indian dishes are especially popular in Dubai, Doha and other Middle Eastern cities, while

Indian and Pakistani restaurants in Saudi Arabia serve pilgrims during the Haj. There are even Indian restaurants in war-torn Kabul that cater to the large number of British and Indian expatriates."

◆◆◆◆◆

It is heartwarming to see that many countries that adopted curry gave it a place of high honor in their cuisines. In these countries—relatively new to curry—curry is often considered by the masses to be either the heart of comfort food or a very special treat to be featured in celebrations and weekly rituals. A significant number of nations identify it as their national dish.

HOW TO NAVIGATE THIS BOOK

The recipes in the following pages highlight countries around the world that celebrate curries. They are broken down by nation within continents. I have never been a fan of using words like *authentic*, *classic*, and *traditional* to describe recipes from different parts of the world. As we have seen time and time again, food is dynamic and is a reflection of the fluidity of cultures that accommodate new ingredients and techniques, or adjusts when ingredients or techniques fall out of favor. I consider the curry recipes representative of a particular culture, but every cook within that nation may well have hundreds of versions. These are my renditions that make use of simple methods and deliver satisfying flavors in your home kitchen (or in a commercial one, for that matter).

1

ASIA

Undeniably, the South Asian subcontinent is the birthplace of curries, its magical prowess unsheathed with hundreds of spices and flavorings at its disposal. Its cooks roast, pulverize, and perfume a seemingly unending array of stews, stir-fries, rice dishes, and breads—all incorporating flavors that span the spice alphabet from amchur to zafran. No surprise this neck of Asia became the epicenter of the world's spice trade, tempting merchants, invaders, and colonizers to its shores. With a whopping forty-eight countries in Asia, it is no easy task to identify each country's desire for a particular array of spices in their culinary repertoire. But the influences of spices, herbs, aromatics, and pastes are deepest felt in the southeast countries of Asia. Like a whirling dervish dancer who spins with dizzying but controlled balance, a cook in Thailand pounds disparate ingredients like lemongrass, lime leaves, fresh galangal, toasted cumin, coriander, and a multicolored array of chilies to fashion a sophisticated and well-nuanced paste with which to punctuate their curries. China's and Japan's reliance on the anglicized curry powder, and Sri Lanka's inclusion of all things related to its native cinnamon, make for many more equally scintillating curries.

THE MOTHER BLEND

Madras curry powder

✦ INDIA AND ENGLAND

19

BUTTER CHICKEN

Murgh makhani ✦ INDIA

22

MINTY DATE-STUFFED LAMB PATTIES with STEWED MUSTARD GREENS

Chapli kebab saag ✦ PAKISTAN

26

MUSTARD-FENNEL SMOTHERED SHAD

Sorshe ilish maacher jhol ✦ BANGLADESH

30

PRAWN CURRY with DARKENED CINNAMON

Aňduru kuruňdu samaňga issan kariya

✦ SRI LANKA

34

POTATO and BAMBOO SHOOT CURRY with BLACK-EYED PEAS

Aloo bodi tama ✦ NEPAL

36

STEAMED TURMERIC- and CHILI-SMOTHERED HALIBUT in BANANA LEAVES

Fish amok ✦ CAMBODIA

39

EGG NOODLE SOUP with COCONUT MILK

Khow suey ✦ MYANMAR

42

THE CURRY PASTE TRILOGY

Kæng kaẖrì ṭir phākh ✦ THAILAND

44

RED CURRY PASTE 46
GREEN CURRY PASTE 47
YELLOW CURRY PASTE 50

PAN-FRIED TOFU with RED CURRY PASTE

Têāẖû p̄ẖạd phrik p̄ẖeā ✦ THAILAND

52

CHICKEN LEMONGRASS CURRY with POTATOES

Cà-ri gà + VIETNAM

55

CURRY NOODLES with SHRIMP

Mee kari dengan udang

+ HONG KONG AND MALAYSIA

58

CHICKEN CURRY with LEMONGRASS and CURRY LEAVES

Kari ayam + MALAYSIA

61

FLAKY GRIDDLE-COOKED BREADS

Roti canai + MALAYSIA AND BEYOND

65

PAN-FRIED SALTED COD CURRY with CUCUMBER RELISH

Bacalhau gulai + BORNEO

68

UNRIPE JACKFRUIT and POTATOES with MUSSELS

Gulai cubadak + INDONESIA

71

WOK-SEARED CURRIED FRIED RICE

Gali fen ch'ao fan + CHINA

75

FLAKY CURRY PUFFS

Piàn zhuàng gālí pào fú + CHINA

77

STEAMED CHICKEN DUMPLINGS with a SPICED TOMATO SAUCE

Momos + TIBET

80

CHICKEN CURRY with CARROTS and PICKLED GINGER

Kare raisu + JAPAN

86

JEWEL IN THE CROWN

Madras curry powder is a perfect example of Britain's colonialist tendency to simplify and package all that was foreign, complex, and "exotic." India, their "jewel in the crown" (which they inhabited, first as traders and then as rulers, from 1608 to 1947), enticed Britain with its aromatic, peppery, complexly layered, 6,000-year-old dishes: There is evidence of mortars and pestles having been used in the 4000 BCE Mohenjo-Daro civilization of the Indus Valley! Indian cooks had a seemingly chaotic way of spicing food—oftentimes roasting, toasting, and pounding a combination of disparate ingredients—but it resulted in flavors that were harmonious, layered, and nuanced.

In *Oxford Companion to Food*, Alan Davidson takes us back to 1885 when Colonel A. R. Kenney-Herbert, a distinguished writer on the foods of the Anglo-Indians, took a stab at a "stock for curry powder." It incorporated turmeric, coriander seed, cumin seed, fenugreek, mustard seed, dried chilies, black peppercorns, poppy seed, and dry ginger—and he offered up the recipe even though commercial curry powder mixtures were being used in Britain at the time.

> **"There is evidence of mortars and pestles having been used in the 4000 BCE Mohenjo-Daro civilization of the Indus Valley!"**

For epochs prior, South Indian cooks were sun-drying these same spices to flavor signature stews called sambhars. A unique combination was fashioned in each home kitchen, defying a homogeneity throughout all South Indian kitchens. However, the British creation of a uniform and good-tasting Anglo-Indian curry gained a foothold and opened the world to Madras curry powder, a simplified adaptation named after South India's coastal city of Madras (now called Chennai).

Yes, you can procure many kinds of Madras curry powders all across the globe in the spice aisle of any supermarket, but making your own is embarrassingly simple, time efficient (you really can't spare five minutes of your time to make this?), and frugal. Here is my version, used in many of the recipes in this book.

The Mother Blend

Madras curry powder ·◆· Makes 1 cup

2 tablespoons coriander seeds (see Tips)

1 tablespoon cumin seeds (see Tips)

2 teaspoons fenugreek seeds

1 teaspoon fennel seeds

1 teaspoon black or yellow mustard seeds

1 teaspoon black peppercorns

½ teaspoon whole cloves

1 teaspoon cardamom seeds (see Tips)

8 to 10 dried red chiles (like chile de arbol), stems discarded

2 sticks cinnamon, broken up into smaller pieces

1 tablespoon ground turmeric

1 teaspoon ground ginger

½ teaspoon freshly grated nutmeg

1 Pile all the ingredients except the turmeric, ginger, and nutmeg in a spice grinder (or a clean coffee grinder). You may have to grind the whole spices in batches if your grinder is unable to accommodate that voluminous pile in one swoop. Grind the ingredients to the consistency of finely ground black pepper, tapping the lid to release any of the intoxicating blend back into the grinder's cavity. Transfer to a medium bowl. Repeat with the remaining whole spices.

2 Stir in the turmeric, ginger, and nutmeg to fashion a blend that may very well draw the word "wowee" from your lips (after the nose does the talking).

3 Store this spice blend in an airtight jar (preferably glass) in your cool, dry pantry, away from sunlight. In my opinion, refrigerating the blend will adversely affect its flavors (because of the moisture in the cooling unit). This blend will keep for up to 6 months.

TIPS

✦ Part of the Apiaceae—also called Umbelliferae—family (think parsley, fennel, and carrot), the coriander plant, indigenous to the Mediterranean region, is known by many names: cilantro, Chinese parsley, and Arab parsley. The leaves and seeds have found extensive usage in food, medicine, and preservation. The Egyptians were using it as early as 1352 BCE and the Buddhist emperor Ashoka introduced it to India around 200 BCE. The lightweight and light-colored brownish-yellow seeds are highly aromatic, very citrus-like, especially when ground fresh. Coriander is a key ingredient in curry powders; I highly recommend buying it only as seeds. (You'll find a lengthier description of eight different flavors of coriander in my 2008 book, *660 Curries*.)

✦ A crucial spice along the spice route, cumin is also a member of the Apiaceae family and is the Mediterranean's gift to the world. Many curry powders and other blends (like Morocco's ras al hanout, used in Slow-Cooked Chickpeas with Saffron on page 106) incorporate this slender, spindle-shaped spice that is musky, nutty, earthy, and highly aromatic.

✦ True cardamom, indigenous to the hilly areas of southwestern India in Kerala, is the second most expensive spice in the world (next to saffron), and its heady menthol-like aromas have won the world over in savory and sweet recipes. A close cousin to ginger and turmeric, these plump green pods (reminding me of bleeding hearts) are hand-picked and sun-dried or spread out on drying racks in small sheds. They are available at Indian markets, some supermarkets, and online; some stores stock the bleached-white version of green pods, and I have found no difference in taste and aroma between them.

✦ To get at the seeds, pry open the pod with your fingers. A whack with the broadside of a knife also helps loosen the pod. Remove the black seeds from within and discard the skin and small vein that holds them together. Pods vary in size but 6 to 8 should yield ½ teaspoon of seeds; you'll need 10 to 12 for a whole teaspoonful.

TAMING THE TANDOOR

It was not love at first sight, my encounter with a commercial tandoor. The clay-lined oven encased in a stainless-steel shell sat atop a gargantuan gas burner, quietly smoldering, seething at almost 700°F, waiting to engulf me in its deepness. I approached gingerly, mounted the metal step, and peeked down into the hot abyss. A searing blast slapped my face, but I fought the strong desire to flee. I was, after all, going to master the tandoor, tame it, make it conform to my commands, and produce those delicious naans and tandoori chickens, the same chickens that would bathe in a buttery cream sauce laced with fenugreek to make butter chicken, a dish that sends people into a culinary ecstasy.

Perhaps this is what Kundan Lal Gujral experienced when he worked as a cook at a former roadside dhaba (truck stop), which also happened to specialize in sweets, in Peshawar (now in Pakistan) during the pre-partition days of the British Raj. He marinated full chickens, skinless, with yogurt, ginger, garlic, and freshly ground spices and then skewered them onto metal rods that rested in the tandoor's cavernous base, red and vibrant, spitting flames from the coals that were dripped with chicken fat. They hung, spread-eagled, on their hot rods, beckoning travelers to sample a phenomenon called tandoori chicken. But as the birds dried in the heat, Gujral, unwilling to waste a single bite, separated the meat from the bones and simmered it in a sauce of pureed tomatoes, butter, cream, and dried fenugreek leaves. And so butter chicken was born. Upon the ending of the British Raj and the partition of India, Gujral and his family moved to Dehli, where he reopened his eatery Moti Mahal in the central district of Delhi called Daryaganj. And, as the old adage goes, the rest is history. Butter chicken spread across the globe and became the iconic curry of India, its succulent sauce cloaking the humble bird in many a chef's pan.

Butter Chicken

Murgh makhani ·•· Serves 4

FOR THE CHICKEN

¼ cup heavy (whipping) cream or half-and-half

2 tablespoons finely chopped fresh ginger

5 medium cloves garlic, finely chopped

1 tablespoon finely chopped fresh cilantro

1 teaspoon coriander seeds, freshly ground

1 teaspoon cumin seeds, freshly ground

½ teaspoon coarse sea salt

¼ teaspoon ground red pepper (cayenne)

1½ pounds boneless skinless chicken breasts

FOR THE SAUCE

1 tablespoon ghee (for homemade, see Variation, page 95) or melted butter (see Tips)

½ cup tomato sauce

2 tablespoons dried fenugreek leaves (see Tips)

½ teaspoon ground red pepper (cayenne)

¼ cup heavy (whipping) cream or half-and-half

Vegetable cooking spray

Naan with ghee, or cooked rice (see page 193), for serving

1 To make the marinade for the chicken, whisk together the cream, ginger, garlic, cilantro, ground coriander and cumin, salt, and ground red pepper in a medium bowl. Add the chicken breasts to the marinade and give it all a good mix, making sure the breasts are well coated. Refrigerate, covered, for at least an hour, preferably overnight.

2 When ready to cook, preheat a gas or charcoal grill, or the broiler, to high.

3 Make the sauce by heating the ghee in a medium saucepan over medium heat. Pour in the tomato sauce, fenugreek leaves, and red pepper. Simmer the sauce, covered, stirring occasionally, to allow the leaves to perfume the sauce, 5 to 8 minutes. Some of the ghee will start to separate from the sauce.

4 Gently pour in the cream, stirring to make a creamy red sauce. Turn off the heat and keep the sauce covered while you cook the chicken.

5 *If you are grilling*, lightly spray the grill grate with vegetable cooking spray. Grill the chicken over indirect heat, covered, turning occasionally, until the breasts are light brown, 15 to 20 minutes. (To test for doneness, slice into a piece with a paring knife; the meat should no longer be pink and the juices should run clear.) *If you are broiling*, position a rack so the top of the chicken will be 2 to 3 inches from the heat. Lightly spray the rack of a broiler pan with cooking spray, place the chicken on the pan, and broil, turning occasionally, until the breasts are light brown, the meat is no longer pink inside, and the juices run clear, 15 to 20 minutes. Transfer the breasts to a cutting board and cut them into 1-inch-wide strips.

(recipe continues)

6 Add the cooked succulent pieces, including any juices, to the sauce, making sure every piece is coated with that luscious sauce. Turn the heat back on to medium and bring the curry to a gentle boil, stirring occasionally, to allow the chicken to absorb the flavors, about 5 minutes. Serve hot with naan, slathered with ghee, right out of a tandoor. I won't judge if you buy the naan premade or even serve the curry with rice.

TIPS

✦ Ideally, which fat to use for the sauce? I prefer the clarity of ghee over milk solid–laden butter. Ghee infuses a nutty quality, parallel to none, plus it is considered way better than butter in terms of healthy attributes. And it is free of lactose.

✦ Fenugreek, also known as Greek hay (since it was fed to cattle in Greece for its ability to help lactating cows produce more milk), is a very important plant in India, Africa (it was used in the tomb of Tutankhamun), and also parts of Europe. The plant has been around for at least 6,000 years and every part of it can be used culinarily as well as for health reasons. With small clover-like leaves, the plant grows close to the ground and needs to be thoroughly washed before use.

✦ Separate the leaves from the stems and dunk them under cool water, swishing them around to allow the dirt to settle to the bottom. Repeat this a few times, changing the water as needed. I characterize the leaves as having a perfumed bitterness, and the seeds, slightly triangular-shaped, are intensely bitter and hard. The seeds are a key inclusion in commercial (and homemade) curry powders; their aroma, almost maple-like, is what gives curry powders that je-ne-sais-quoi quality. Fresh leaves are often used as an herb as well as greens (like you would spinach or mustard greens). When dried, they are labeled as kasoori methi, and it's in this form that they bring butter chicken to life. If the sauce has no dried fenugreek leaves, it ain't butter chicken in my book.

A NATION DIVIDED

The forceful partition of India in 1947, a result of the culmination of the British Raj, established Pakistan, a country that remains predominantly Muslim, including its culture and cuisine. The area that is Pakistan thrived during the height of the Harappan civilization around 2500 BCE in the basins of the Indus River. Its contemporary cuisine is a reflection of the presence of the Mughal Empire (early sixteenth to mid-nineteenth-century CE), rich with aromatic spices, dried fruits, and nuts. Meats and poultry feature prominently in their daily meals, and dishes like haleem (a wheat- and meat-based curry), paya (a rich stew with goat trotters), and korma (nut-based saucy dishes with saffron) are well loved. Mustard greens, black-eyed peas, bitter melon, and lentils shore up their diets, many dishes being punctuated with ginger, garlic, onion, tomatoes, and spices that deliver strong flavors and aromas.

What is particularly endearing to many Pakistanis is the cuisine of Peshawar in the northern and northwestern region of the country, an area in close proximity to Afghanistan, sharing the latter's penchant for nuts and dried fruits in many of their meat-based dishes. Vegetables have a short growing season, so their usage is maximized.

"**Mustard greens, black-eyed peas, bitter melon, and lentils shore up their diets.**"

These lamb patties, also known as Peshawari or chapli kebabs, always incorporate nuts in some form or the other. My version includes ground, blanched almonds that provide not only flavor, but also a binding quality that holds the patties together as you pan-fry them. A little surprise of dates in their center creates a wow factor and when you serve them alongside a stew of minty mustard greens, the result is nothing short of memorable.

Minty Date-Stuffed Lamb Patties with Stewed Mustard Greens

Chapli kebab saag ·•· Serves 4

FOR THE LAMB PATTIES

1 pound ground lamb

¼ cup ground blanched almonds

1 teaspoon garam masala (see Tip, page 191)

1 teaspoon ground fennel seeds

1 teaspoon coarse sea salt

½ teaspoon ground red pepper (cayenne)

¼ cup finely chopped red onion

¼ cup finely chopped fresh mint leaves

2 large cloves garlic, finely chopped

6 medium to large pitted dates (like Medjool), finely chopped

1 tablespoon canola oil

FOR THE STEWED MUSTARD GREENS

2 tablespoons mustard or canola oil

1 teaspoon cumin seeds

1 teaspoon fennel seeds

4 large cloves garlic, coarsely chopped

2 dried red Thai or cayenne chilies, stems removed

1 pound fresh mustard greens, coarsely chopped (see Tips)

½ cup firmly packed fresh mint leaves

2 tablespoons coarsely chopped fresh dill

1 teaspoon coarse sea salt

2 tablespoons ghee (for homemade, see Variation, page 95) or butter, plus extra for serving (optional)

2 tablespoons ground blanched almonds

Juice of 1 medium lime

1 To make the patties, thoroughly combine the lamb, almonds, garam masala, fennel, salt, ground red pepper, onion, mint, and garlic in a medium bowl. Divide into 4 equal portions.

2 Working with one portion of lamb at a time, shape it into a round. Then press the round into a disc roughly 2 inches in diameter. With your finger make a dimple-like (yes, I have dimples) indentation in its center and place a tablespoon of the chopped dates in it. Gather the edges and fold them over the filling and reshape it into a patty roughly 1 inch thick. Repeat with the remaining lamb and dates. Refrigerate them until you are ready to eat, for up to 2 days.

3 Meanwhile, make the stewed mustard greens. Heat the 2 tablespoons of oil in a large saucepan or skillet over medium-high heat. Once the oil appears to shimmer, add the cumin and fennel seeds and let them sizzle, turn reddish brown, and become aromatic, 5 to 10 seconds. Immediately throw in the garlic and the chilies. Stir-fry to take the raw edge off the garlic and to slightly blacken the chilies, 1 to 2 minutes.

4 A handful at a time, drop the mustard greens into the spiced oil and stir-fry until they wilt. Repeat until all the greens have been added and wilted. Stir in the mint leaves and dill. Continue to cook the greens, uncovered, stirring occasionally, until their liquid evaporates and leaves a slight sheen on the leaves, 8 to 12 minutes. Stir in the salt.

(recipe continues)

TIPS

✦ Mustard greens, also known as mustard spinach, belong in a class of their own, with a staggering array of varieties ranging from flat-leaf to curly, tender to tough, fibrous to smooth, highly bitter to mellow, and green to burgundy. Native to the Central Himalayan regions (more than 5,000 years back), these greens are nutritional powerhouses with high amounts of dietary iron, and are prized in many parts of the world because of their depth of flavor and bitterness (a sought-after taste element in numerous cultures to provide a layered balance to many dishes). With the exception of the southern part of the United States, they are not especially popular elsewhere in North America. Non-European cultures use them with much regularity, spices often balancing out the bitterness to yield nuanced results. For the most part (with the exception of farmers' markets and Asian supermarkets), your favorite grocery store will carry only one variety.

✦ To prepare the greens for cooking, discard the tough ribs that run almost halfway through the centers. Stack a few leaves atop one another and roll them into a cylinder. Thinly slice the cylinder crosswise into strips (for this recipe, then coarsely chop them) and transfer them to a large bowl filled with cold water. Repeat the stacking and slicing (or chopping) process with the remaining leaves. Once all the leaves are prepped, swish them around in the water and allow any dirt and grit to settle to the bottom. Grab handfuls of the washed leaves without shaking them again and let them drip in a colander. Empty the bowl of water and refill it with cold water. Repeat the dunking, swishing, and emptying the water at least twice more to make sure the water left behind in the bowl is clean and devoid of any grit. Pat the leaves a bit with paper towels to rid them of excess moisture before cooking.

5 Pour in 2 cups water, scraping the pan to deglaze it, releasing any browned bits of spice and greens. Bring to a boil. Then lower the heat to medium, cover the pan, and simmer, stirring occasionally, until the greens are tender and olive green, about 15 minutes. Remove the pan from the heat.

6 Transfer the greens, liquid and all, to a blender jar. Puree, scraping the inside of the jar as needed, to make a smooth puree. Return the puree to the pan, and fold in the 2 tablespoons ghee and the ground almonds. Place the pan over low heat, cover, and cook, stirring the greens occasionally, until the almonds have absorbed some of the liquid liquid and the mixture has thickened, about 15 minutes. Continue to cook them, now uncovered, to allow some of the excess liquid to dissipate and provide an added depth to the greens, 8 to 10 minutes. Fold in the lime juice and transfer the puree to a serving bowl.

7 Now, before you pan-fry the lamb patties, line a plate with paper towels.

8 Heat the tablespoon of oil in a large nonstick or cast-iron skillet over medium heat. Once the oil appears to shimmer, place the 4 lamb patties in the pan and allow them to sizzle and sear on the undersides, about 1 minute. Then place a lid on the skillet and continue to cook the patties until the undersides are evenly dark brown, 3 to 4 minutes. Flip the patties over and repeat the searing and covered cooking on the other side, 3 to 4 minutes more. You want the meat to be slightly pink (medium) in the center. Lift them off the skillet onto the paper towel–lined plate to drain the excess fat.

9 Serve the lamb patties warm with the mustard greens (saag). If you like, pass extra ghee to drizzle atop the tart, slightly bitter, nutty-tasting saag for added succulence.

THE BACKYARDS OF THE BENGALIS

When the British were forced to leave India in 1947, after their more than 300-year presence, they divided the nation into India, West Pakistan, and East Pakistan upon their exit. The partition resulted in millions of displaced households and thousands of fatalities. Twenty-five years later, at the culmination of a conflict with India, East Pakistan (containing the province East Bengal) was granted its own nation status with the new name Bangladesh ("the land of the Bengalis").

My own memory of the war is vivid. In 1971, India and Pakistan declared war over the possession of East Bengal. We sat in near blackness in our flat's dining room in suburban Andheri (a prescient name, one derived from the Hindi word *andher*, meaning "darkness") in what was then known as Bombay (now Mumbai). Once dusk settled in against the horizon, Bombay residents were forbidden from turning on lights. Blackouts were essential to appearing invisible to the "other side" should any Pakistani bomber plane pass over India's unfriendly skies. All the windows in our apartment were covered with black blotting paper, imprisoning the yellow brilliance of a single oil lamp sitting one foot high on the terrazzo floor. The light danced with the grace of a Bharatanatyam dancer, casting wavelike shadows on the room's walls. We spoke in hushed voices in fear that the bombers would hear us from their high-altitude mission.

The frequent, dulled swoosh of passing planes, muffled by the thickly papered windows, mixed in with our feather-soft voices as we ate a simple meal in darkness. Rice, a staple in our Tamil kitchen, was a rare commodity during these warring times. Rains were unusually scarce that year and the meager grains were reserved for the soldiers in this battlefield of neighbors agitated by religious zealots on both sides. As kitchen staples were rationed nationwide, I wondered about the kitchens of East Bengal, whose people were avid eaters of rice alongside fish—in particular, a variety called hilsa or ilish, a silver freshwater fish that spawns in the eastern waters and populated their aromatic-sour curries. While we comforted ourselves with Tamil fare in Mumbai, I hoped for the same well-being for those other families in their war-torn backyards.

Mustard-Fennel Smothered Shad

Sorshe ilish maacher jhol ⋅➤⋅ Serves 4

1 teaspoon fennel seeds

1 teaspoon cumin seeds

1 teaspoon black or yellow mustard seeds

1 teaspoon nigella seeds (see Tips)

4 dried red chiles (like chile de arbol), stems removed

½ teaspoon ground turmeric

1 teaspoon coarse sea salt

2 tablespoons mustard oil or canola oil (see Tips)

1 small yellow onion, finely chopped

4 large cloves garlic, finely chopped

4 skinless fillets (about 6 ounces each) bluefish, buffalo fish, bass, or other firm-fleshed white fish (if using hilsa, see Tips)

1 large tomato, cored and finely chopped

2 tablespoons finely chopped fresh cilantro

1 Pile the fennel, cumin, mustard, and nigella seeds along with the red chiles into the bowl of a spice grinder (or clean coffee grinder). Pulverize the mélange into a blend with the consistency of finely ground black pepper. Tap the lid to release any of the intoxicating blend back into the grinder's cavity. Transfer to a small bowl and stir in the turmeric and salt. Pour ¼ cup water over the blend and mix it into a thick slurry, mottled with shades of yellow, red, and brown.

2 Heat the mustard oil in a large skillet over medium-high heat. This amber-colored oil, pungent beyond words, will elicit tears once it starts to simmer. This is when you add the onion and garlic (also piquant ingredients) and stir-fry the medley until it turns light brown around the edges, surprisingly taming down the potency, 2 to 3 minutes.

3 Now scrape the slurry into the pan and continue to cook, uncovered, stirring occasionally, until the water evaporates and the oils from the spices form a glistening sheen on the slightly chunky base for the fish curry, about 5 minutes.

4 Place the fillets atop the base, making sure to spoon some of it over the fish. Spread the tomato pieces on top and cover the pan. Lower the heat to medium and let the fish bathe in all that goodness, 3 to 4 minutes. Flip the fillets over and make sure they get cloaked in the chunky sauce. Cover the pan and continue to poach the fish until it barely starts to flake, 3 to 4 more minutes.

5 Serve the fillets warm sprinkled with the cilantro.

TIPS

✦ Nigella seeds, called kalonji in Bangladesh and India, are not onion seeds (as they are often mistakenly identified), nor are they named after the food-television personality. Instead, they are the seeds of the *Nigella sativa* plant in the family Ranunculaceae. Nigella seeds and onion seeds look similar with their jet-black, almost triangular-shaped appearance, so you can see why there is confusion. Many Middle Eastern and Armenian bakers dot their breads with the seeds of nigella. They are available online as well as at any store that stocks groceries from the Indian subcontinent.

✦ A cash crop that dates back 6,000 years in India, mustard, a member of the Brassica family (think cabbage, cauliflower, broccoli, and, yes, even canola), is a prized commodity in the cuisine of Bangladesh and many parts of India as well. Mustard in all its forms is revered and many dishes include mustard seeds and mustard oil in one bitter swoop. Yes, mustard's individuality may seem obtrusive to the palate, but when balanced with the right spices and herbs, the resulting dishes are transformative and magical. Pure mustard oil is a viscous, deep amber–colored liquid and a whiff of it makes you question its inclusion. Pure extracted oil, from the seeds of the juncea variety of mustard, is marked as "for external use only" on labels here in the United States, because of the presence of the toxic erucic acid, considered unsafe for human consumption. Tell that to the people of Bangladesh and the surrounding regions who have not died from it even after thousands of years of use. In the United States, it is often sold in bottles mixed with a mild-tasting vegetable or soybean oil, making it safer for cooking. Whatever your choice, mustard oil does make a strong and desirable presence in this curry, and many others.

✦ A freshwater fish, the hilsa (ilish maach in Bengali) or the hilsa shad is rarely found fresh in the United States, even in Indian or South Asian grocery stores that carry otherwise hard-to-find ingredients. Bangladesh remains the world's largest producer of hilsa, an oily fish related to herring, rich with omega-3 fatty acids. In their curries, the fish is cleaned and cut into serving-size pieces, skin, bones, and all. It takes dexterity, especially when eating with your fingers, to separate the skin from the meat and eat around the multitude of sharp bones. But the sweet-tender meat makes the work worthwhile. Two of the more comparable and easily available substitutes are the bluefish and buffalo fish, both known for their oiliness, strong flavor, and medium-firm texture (you'll want skinless fillets). US-farmed bass makes a sustainable alternative, if the bluefish or the buffalo fish are not as readily available.

THE CINNAMON TRAIL

This tear-shaped island just south of India has had so much history, topographical variety, internal conflict, and culinary crosspollination crammed into its relatively small size. Sri Lanka's proximity to India is like a tether that has held the two countries together for thousands of years, bound by religion, strife, colonies, and spices. A mellifluous array of curries marks the distinctive style of Sri Lankan food, a reflection of the Portuguese, Dutch, and English who colonized the island for more than 130 years. And let's not forget the influence of the Scottish tea growers, Muslims, Malaysians, and Moors.

I was fortunate to spend time in Sri Lanka (formerly Ceylon) leading groups on food and cultural tours to the southern half of the country. The northern, northwestern, and coastal eastern regions still felt unsettled after the long civil war that devastated the island between 1983 and 2009, a conflict between the Hindu Tamil Tigers and the Buddhist Sinhalese. I experienced a culinary artist's tapestry of red, white, and black curries, ranging from mellow coconut meat and milk to assertive dishes with red chilies to those interlaced with spices like coriander, fenugreek, cloves, and cinnamon, darkly toasted and highly intoxicating.

Southern Sri Lanka boasts of cultivating true cinnamon. Dr. Darin Gunesekera, a social entrepreneur living in Sri Lanka's largest city, Colombo, led us to Puhulwella in southern Sri Lanka, home to a cinnamon plantation he runs, which employs women from impoverished neighboring homes and uses only sustainable and ethical practices. I witnessed the harvesting of the cinnamon trees with their pink-hued red leaves, their slender barks stripped and naturally furled as they dried, scenting the space with their sweetness. Later we supped on home-cooked curries, hot sambals, red rice, lacy-edged crepe-like rice hoppers, and noodles, all washed down with coconut water—an experience evoked in this recipe.

TIPS

✦ Never buy ground cinnamon, as the oils in it dissipate in aroma and flavor. You are far better off grinding the whole sticks just before use.

✦ Fresh curry leaves provide a mild citrusy flavor and intense aroma—find them at Indian groceries and online. Remove the leaves by sliding your fingers down the stem.

Prawn Curry
with Darkened Cinnamon

Aňduru kuruňdu samaňga issan kariya ◦ Serves 4

3 sticks cinnamon (see Tips)

2 teaspoons Madras Curry Powder (page 19)

6 medium cloves garlic, finely chopped

3 slices fresh ginger (each about the size of a quarter), finely chopped

1 pound large shrimp (21 to 25 per pound), peeled and deveined, but tails left on

2 tablespoons coconut or canola oil

1 teaspoon black or yellow mustard seeds

1 can (14 ounces) unsweetened coconut milk

¼ cup coarsely chopped fresh curry leaves (see Tips)

2 teaspoons black peppercorns, coarsely cracked

1 teaspoon coarse sea salt

1 Preheat a small skillet over medium-high heat. Once the pan is hot (holding your palm close to the base, you should feel the heat within 5 seconds), break up the cinnamon sticks into smaller pieces (for an even toast) and throw them in the skillet. Toast, stirring the pieces constantly, or shaking the skillet very often, until they darken further and smell incredibly fragrant, 1 to 2 minutes. Transfer them to a spice grinder (or clean coffee grinder), and allow the pieces to cool, about 5 minutes. Pulverize the cinnamon to the texture of finely ground black pepper.

2 Combine the cinnamon, curry powder, garlic, and ginger in a large bowl; add the shrimp and toss to coat. Refrigerate, covered, for at least 30 minutes or as long as overnight.

3 Heat the oil in a large skillet over medium-high heat. Once the oil appears to shimmer, add the mustard seeds, cover, and cook until the seeds have stopped popping, about 30 seconds. Immediately add the shrimp in a single layer, and sear them for about 30 seconds on each side.

4 Shake the coconut milk well and pour it in. Add the curry leaves, peppercorns, and salt. Bring the curry to a boil and continue to cook until the shrimp curl and turn salmon in color, 3 to 5 minutes. Using a slotted spoon, transfer the shrimp to a serving platter. Keep warm.

5 Continue to cook the sauce, uncovered, stirring occasionally, until it has thickened, 2 to 4 minutes. Spoon the sauce over the shrimp and serve.

LAND OF THE HIMALAYAS

The birthplace of Gautama Buddha, landlocked Nepal is nestled partly in the Himalayan mountains and surrounded by big countries like China, India, Bhutan, and Tibet. The country was never colonized but did serve as a go-between for British India and Imperial China. Northern Nepal is more in touch with Tibet's culture (in fact, Nepal has a very large community of Tibetan immigrants and refugees), while the southern region embraces some of India's cooking techniques, especially in the use of legumes and vegetables. Nepal's spicing techniques are not as ornate and orchestrated as India's, but the simplicity of their curries in showcasing local ingredients is evident, especially the cuisine of Newar in the central Kathmandu Valley, home of the traders who were influential along the Silk Road. Nepali kitchens put out meals that are uncluttered and satisfying. Local mustard greens make a daily appearance as do rice and dal.

I was fortunate to be in the capital city of Kathmandu in 2014, the year before its major earthquake. A riot of colors, a frenzied marketplace, naked chickens bathed in yogurt and spices roasting on an open fire, gunnysacks overflowing with legumes, sidewalks splashed with piles of fenugreek greens and marigolds, sleeping dogs under prayer wheels—all came together in this city's marketplace along the silk route.

Growing up in Kathmandu, Naveen Shrestha had no inkling that one day he would become a cook and restaurant owner in the United States. He was busy being a hotel clerk, taking care of his mother, brother, and sister-in-law. Once he turned twenty-five, he had the opportunity to emigrate to the United States, and in 1996, he landed in San Francisco to start a new life. Within months, a family friend beckoned him to Minnesota, and he immediately fell in love with its climate, people, and way of life. After all, he was used to the cold, having lived in the mountainous areas of Nepal.

His journey into the restaurant world began at a local grill, where he learned to cook the American way. His reliable clientele was curious about his fare from Nepal, something different from the regular menu of eggs, burgers, and salads. After gaining confidence cooking foods from his childhood, he eventually opened his own restaurant, aptly named Himalayan, in 2008. This is where I sampled aloo bodi tama, a popular Nepali curry featuring potatoes, bamboo shoots, mustard greens, and black-eyed peas. Here is my version.

Potato and Bamboo Shoot Curry with Black-Eyed Peas

Aloo bodi tama ⋅⋆⋅ Serves 6

1 cup dried black-eyed peas (see Tips)

1 bunch (12 to 16 ounces) mustard greens

1 small red onion, coarsely chopped

6 medium cloves garlic, peeled

2 fresh green serrano chiles, stems removed

2 tablespoons ghee (for homemade, see Variation, page 95) or canola oil

2 teaspoons unrefined brown or white sugar

1½ teaspoons coarse sea salt

2 tablespoons coriander seeds, ground

1 teaspoon cumin seeds, ground

1 teaspoon sweet Hungarian paprika or ground annatto (achiote) seeds

½ teaspoon ground turmeric

1 large tomato, cored, and finely chopped

2 medium red-skin potatoes, peeled and cut into 1-inch cubes (see Tips)

1 can (15 ounces) bamboo shoots, drained

Juice from 1 large lime

1 Place the peas in a pressure cooker. Fill the cooker halfway with tap water and rinse the peas by rubbing them between your fingertips. The water may appear slightly dirty. Drain this water. Repeat three or four times until the water, after rinsing, is relatively clear; drain. Now add 4 cups water and bring to a boil, uncovered, over high heat. Skim and discard any foam that surfaces to the top. Seal the cooker shut and allow the pressure to build up. Once the bell-shaped weight begins to jiggle or whistle, lower the heat to medium-low, and cook for about 20 minutes. Turn off the burner and allow the pressure to subside naturally before opening the lid, about 15 minutes.

2 While the peas cook, cut the mustard greens into chiffonade and rinse thoroughly (see Tips, page 27). Set aside.

3 Pile the onion, garlic, and chiles in a food processor bowl and, using the pulsing action, mince the mélange to make a pungent, eye-stinging blend.

4 Heat the ghee in a large skillet over medium heat. Scrape the minced blend into the skillet and stir-fry until earthy brown, 10 to 12 minutes.

5 Stir in the sugar, salt, coriander, cumin, paprika, and turmeric. The heat in the browned onion medley is just right to cook the spices without burning them, about 30 seconds.

6 Dump in the mustard greens, tomato, and potatoes. Simmer, uncovered, stirring occasionally, to soften the tomato and partially cook the perfumed, slightly bitter mustard greens and the potatoes, about 5 minutes.

7 Once the peas are tender, scrape this Christmassy-looking red-and-green mélange into the peas along with the bamboo shoots. Simmer the curry in the pressure cooker, uncovered, on medium heat, stirring occasionally, to flavor the peas and cook the potatoes until fork-tender, about 10 minutes.

8 Stir in the lime juice and serve warm.

TIPS

➤ If you do not wish to cook black-eyed peas from scratch, frozen black-eyed peas are a perfectly acceptable alternative. Follow the package directions to cook them. If you use canned black-eyed peas (2 cans, 15 ounces each), make sure you drain and rinse them before use. In both cases, skip Step 1 and in Step 7, scrape the mustard green mixture into a Dutch oven, add the cooked black-eyed peas and 2 cups of water (or cooking liquid, if using frozen), and simmer over medium heat as directed.

➤ Keep the chopped potatoes submerged in a bowl of water and drain just before use.

THE SCENT OF CAMBODIA

Snugly nestled among Thailand, Laos, Vietnam, and the Gulf of Thailand, Cambodia is rich with plains and rivers that have witnessed more than their fair share of traders, colonizers, oppressive regimes, and wars, and it is home to the impressive temple complex called Angkor Wat. During the third century BCE, Cambodia experienced the start of the Buddhist expansion and its monasteries, which preached a particular culinary lifestyle, along with Indian merchants who traded cinnamon, cloves, nutmeg, mace, and peppercorns. Flavors that punctuated curries from Thailand, like galangal, ginger, lemongrass, shallots, and turmeric, were hungrily adopted by the Cambodians. Their colored curry pastes (red, green, and yellow) reflected those of Thailand (see page 44). Beef or duck curries, called samara, marked special celebrations. Scented with cardamom, ginger, peanuts, and other flavorings, these rich curries anchored side dishes of greens, pickles, and condiments.

> **"Flavors that punctuated curries from Thailand, like galangal, ginger, lemongrass, shallots, and turmeric, were hungrily adopted by the Cambodians."**

Seafood especially was and is held dear in Cambodian daily offerings, and this particular custard-like curry, steamed in boats made from banana leaves, has iconic status as the country's national dish, amok. The delicate scent of steaming banana leaves infuses a nuanced aroma and flavor into the curry, which is served with hunks of baguette, a legacy left behind by the French colonizers who populated the country for ninety years beginning in 1863. Do the same if you wish, but I have a soft corner for aromatic jasmine rice as this curry's perfect consort.

Steamed Turmeric- and Chili-Smothered Halibut in Banana Leaves

Fish amok ⟶ Serves 4

1 banana leaf, cut into 4 rectangles and prepped (see Tips)

1½ pounds skinless fillets of halibut, sole, flounder, haddock, cod, whiting, or similar fish

1 cup unsweetened coconut milk

2 tablespoons Yellow Curry Paste (page 50)

1 teaspoon coarse sea salt

1 tablespoon fish sauce

1 large egg, slightly beaten

2 scallions, trimmed, white bulbs and green tops thinly sliced (keep them separate)

1 or 2 fresh Thai red chilies, stems removed, thinly cut along their length into matchstick-thin shreds (do not discard the seeds)

2 cups cooked white jasmine rice (see page 193)

1 Fashion the banana leaves into individual "boats": Working with one leaf rectangle at a time, fold it along a short side, sewing the ends together with a toothpick to secure the fold in place. Repeat with the opposite sides. You now have a canoe-shaped leaf with a generous cavity to hold the curry. Repeat with the remaining leaf rectangles to form four boats.

2 Slice the fish fillets at a diagonal into 1-inch-thick slices and place them in a medium bowl. Quickly whisk together the coconut milk, curry paste, salt, fish sauce, and egg in a small bowl. Pour this mixture over the fish, giving it all a good toss. Allow the fish to marinate in the flavors, 15 to 20 minutes.

3 Meanwhile, get the steamer basket ready. Fill a saucepan halfway with water, insert a steamer basket, and bring the water to a boil. (Or fill a wok halfway with water, set a bamboo steamer in it, and bring the water to a boil.)

4 Prepare the boats for steaming by laying a bed of the white scallion bulbs in each of them. Divide the marinated fish and the sauce equally as well among the four boats. Place the boats carefully in the steamer basket and steam them until the fish barely starts to flake and the sauce thickens a bit, custard-like (thanks to the egg), 10 to 15 minutes.

5 Carefully lift the boats from the steamer basket and serve them topped with the scallion greens and the chilies alongside bowls of steeped jasmine rice.

TIPS

✦ Nothing screams tropical more than bananas, burgundy banana blossoms, and their sprightly green leaves, all of which have been known to exist in rainy, warm climates for more than 10,000 years. Every part of the tree plays a crucial role in some of the Asian and other tropical cultures, its leaves in particular being used to decorate wedding halls and house all kinds of foods that are wrapped, steamed, baked, and grilled. In North America, especially in Florida, these trees are aplenty, so finding fresh leaves is a cinch there. But elsewhere, look for the mature leaves in the freezer section of your Asian supermarket or Latin grocery store. Thaw them and use them as the recipe instructs you. They're as good as the fresh leaves.

✦ Using collard or turnip greens is an acceptable alternative, but do keep in mind they will impart a mellow bitterness to the dish (nothing obtrusive). If using these, make sure each is large enough to fashion a "boat."

✦ To prep the leaves, fill a large saucepan halfway with water and bring it to a rolling boil. Fill a medium to large bowl with cold water, and set it near the stove. Meanwhile, trim off and discard the tough bottom inch of the leaves' ribs (especially if you use collard or turnip greens) to make a rough rectangular shape. Dunk the leaves in the boiling water to soften them, 1 to 2 minutes. Remove them from the hot water and immerse them in the cold water to cool them off quickly. Drain the leaves in a colander. (Alternatively, if you have a gas flame, hold the leaves either with tongs or bare hands—if you have asbestos fingers like mine—and pass them one at a time over the flame. The leaves will change color from an olive green to a bright green, turning flexible and pliant in the process.)

MY HUSBAND WENT TO RANGOON . . .

It would have been blasphemous of me to bypass Myanmar (formerly known as Burma) in this global review of curry's cross-pollination. The cuisine of Myanmar is still often lovingly referred to as Burmese cuisine—a lexical habit that many find pointless to break. Burmese food has strong cultural, religious, and culinary ties to India and, like India, Burma was also an open-bordered country within Britain's South Asian colony. With the early Sakya warriors from India who settled in Burma (around 250 BCE), and the large exodus of Indian laborers after the Anglo-Burmese wars in 1824–1826 and 1886, curries and the role of spices and flavorings became a huge part of Burmese cuisine.

The nation's foods were and are influenced by more than 100 ethnic groups, including those who settled there from the neighboring countries of India, China, and Thailand. The food habits of the Shan people, from the area close to China, reflect China's propensity for soy sauce and a relatively light hand with spices. The region closer to Thailand showcases soupy curries, punctuated with curry pastes and fish sauce. India's proximity influenced the country's street foods in the shape of samosas, perfumed rice biryanis studded with whole spices, and the use of cumin, coriander, star anise, lemongrass, and basil.

Even though coconut milk curries are not as popular in Myanmar as in Thailand and southwest India, its khow suey is a cornucopia of noodles and chicken, blanketed with an assertive curry paste, swimming in rich coconut milk, and topped with an astounding array of vegetables, herbs, and eggs. The real-deal meal that appeals to my way of eating the rainbow! Ironically, this soup made it back to the former Burma with the Indians who emigrated after World War II. There it takes the form of a street food that swirls in many layers of spices and chiles—a confluence of ingredients and flavors emblematic of the two countries' connection. No wonder I loved the old Bollywood melody where a wife croons about her husband's departure to Rangoon (its university used to be populated mostly with people of Indian descent) from where he telephoned her, each confessing the emptiness in their flaming hearts.

Egg Noodle Soup with Coconut Milk

Khow suey ·◆· Serves 4

FOR THE CURRY

1 pound boneless skinless chicken breast, cut into ½-inch cubes

2 tablespoons Yellow Curry Paste (page 50)

2 tablespoons canola oil

2 cans (about 14 ounces each) unsweetened coconut milk

8 to 10 medium to large fresh curry leaves

1 teaspoon coarse sea salt

Juice from 1 medium lime

FOR THE ACCOUTREMENTS

¼ cup canola oil

2 large shallots, thinly sliced and separated

4 large cloves garlic, thinly sliced

2 scallions, trimmed, and thinly sliced (white bulbs and green tops)

1 serrano chile, stem removed, cut in half lengthwise and thinly sliced into half-moons (do not discard the seeds)

2 tablespoons finely chopped fresh cilantro

2 large hard-boiled eggs, cooled, peeled, and cut into 4 pieces each (see page 136)

1 large lime, cut into 4 wedges

FOR THE NOODLES

1 pound fresh egg noodles (see Note)

1 Combine the chicken with the curry paste and give it all a good mix to ensure an even coat around the cubes.

2 Heat the oil in a medium saucepan over medium-high heat. Once the oil appears to shimmer, add the meat and start stir-frying the cubes to sear and brown them, making sure you have adequate ventilation, 5 to 6 minutes.

3 Pour ½ cup water into the pan and scrape the bottom to release collected bits of paste and chicken, effectively deglazing the pan. Shake the coconut milk well, pour it into the pan, and give it all a good stir. Once the curry starts to boil, stir in the curry leaves and salt. Lower the heat to medium-low and briskly simmer, covered, stirring occasionally, until the chicken pieces, when pierced with a fork, release a clear liquid, 8 to 10 minutes. Turn off the heat, stir in the lime juice, and let the pan sit covered as you prepare the accoutrements and the noodles.

4 Grab a couple of paper towels and layer them on a plate. Heat the ¼ cup of canola oil in a small skillet over medium heat. Once the oil appears to shimmer, disperse the shallot slices in the oil. Keep stirring them gently to allow for an even sunny to dark brown disposition, 4 to 6 minutes. With a slotted spoon, lift the slices onto the paper towels.

5 To the oil left behind in the skillet, add the garlic slices and stir-fry them as well until they are earthy brown and crispy, 3 to 5 minutes. Make a little room on the paper towels and add the garlic slices to drain as well.

6 Place the shallots and garlic and the other prepped ingredients for the toppings in separate small to medium bowls.

7 Bring a large saucepan filled three-quarters with water to a rolling boil over medium-high heat. Cook the noodles per the package's instructions (shouldn't be more than 5 minutes or so) until they are just tender (not mushy). Drain them in a colander and give it a good shake or two to rid the noodles of excess water. Divvy them up into four serving bowls.

8 Pour the chicken curry over the noodles to amply cover them. Serve hot and pass around the accoutrements for folks to top their curry as they please.

✦ *I find great success in procuring those fresh egg noodles at any supermarket that stocks groceries from Southeast Asian countries, usually in the fresh produce aisle. For this recipe, use the ones that are slightly thinner than spaghetti.*

VARIATION

Make the curry vegetarian by eliminating the chicken and using 3 cups of cut-up assorted vegetables that are seasonal and that appeal to you.

THE CURRY PASTE TRILOGY

Kæng kaȟrȋ tịr phākh

I am going to go out on a limb and say that Thailand is the only country outside of India to worship curries with such devotion. Cushioned from Myanmar to the west, Laos and Cambodia to the east, and Malaysia to the south, Thailand has a history that goes back to the first century BCE. To understand the influence of India in Thailand, witness the stronghold of the Khmer (aka Angkor) empire (now called Cambodia), from 802 to 1431 CE, which included Thailand and many of the neighboring countries. Hinduism and Buddhism were the main religions that fueled this empire, and stories of Rama and Buddha became its soul. Brahmin priests played the messengers between the kings and the Hindu gods, while traders from India and China peddled in terrestrial goods: spices, opium, sandalwood, silks, tea, and gold.

The foods in Thailand evolved over the centuries from the simplicity of glutinous rice, soy beans, and wild greens among the Indigenous mountain tribes of Khmer that included Hmong, Mien, and Akha (there is an engaging work of historical fiction called *The Tea Girl of Hummingbird Lane* by Lisa See that sheds light on the hardships and uncluttered lives of this community) to a rustic curry paste of galangal, shallots, and peppercorns alongside ferns, wild field greens, pork, frogs, seafood, fowl, and wild deer. As Thailand prospered, so did its cuisine. David Thompson, in his seminal book *Thai Food*, spoke about Nicolas Gervaise, a French Jesuit missionary in the late seventeenth century who, in his book *The Natural and Political History of the Kingdom of Siam*, mused about foods in Thailand: "They mix with all their stews a certain paste made of rotten prawns, called capy in Thai, which has a pungent smell that nauseates anyone not accustomed to it. It is said to give meat a certain zest which whets the appetite . . . so that to make a good sauce in the Siamese manner salt, pepper, ginger, cinnamon, cloves, garlic, white onions, nutmeg and several strongly flavoured herbs must be mixed in considerable quantities with this shrimp

> **"I am going to go out on a limb and say that Thailand is the only country outside of India to worship curries with such devotion."**

paste. At banquets the dishes are served all higgledy-piggledy and in no particular order, with fruit and rice in vessels of gold, silver and porcelain." This is an un-anthropological view, in my not-so-humble opinion. He never understood the role of balance in the world of sophisticated curries and its accoutrements (yes, that's a French word!) from Thailand.

Just as India has a mastery of combining various spices and herbs to fashion their curries, so do modern-day Thai cooks with their curry pastes that form the soul of their regional curries. The country's geographical location is reflected in their provincial curries as Myanmar influences northern pastes (less coconut milk, more spices), while India, Indonesia, and Malaysia inspire southern pastes that are punctuated with cardamom, coconut milk, and cumin. As traders, from the seventeenth to the nineteenth century, the Portuguese upped the curry paste game with their introduction of chiles in the sixteenth century. Praise be!

Here are three curry pastes that reflect amalgamations from various regions of Thailand. They are all complex-tasting, highly nuanced, and easy to make, and will enliven any combination of meats, vegetables, and grains.

Red Curry Paste

Makes ½ cup

1 tablespoon coriander seeds

1 teaspoon cumin seeds

3 small shallots (each the size of a walnut), coarsely chopped

8 to 10 fresh red Thai chilies, stems removed (see Tips, page 48)

1 stalk lemongrass (lower 3 inches), coarsely chopped

3 pieces (each the size of a quarter) fresh galangal (see Tips, page 48)

2 medium fresh lime leaves, middle rib stripped (see Tips, page 48)

1 tablespoon shrimp paste or brown soybean paste (see Tips, page 48)

1 Preheat a small skillet over medium-high heat. Once the pan is at the right temperature (usually takes 2 to 3 minutes), sprinkle in the coriander and cumin. Shake the skillet or use a spoon to stir the seeds around frequently to an even reddish-brown color with a scintillating aroma, 1 to 2 minutes. Transfer the seeds to a small bowl or plate to cool. Once cool to the touch, transfer them to a spice grinder (or clean coffee grinder) and pulverize them until they have the texture of finely ground black pepper.

2 Pile the shallots, chilies, lemongrass, galangal, and lime leaves into the bowl of a food processor. Pulse the ingredients to a coarse paste. At this point I usually like to transfer the mixture to a mortar and pound it into a smoother paste with a pestle, using a spatula to contain it in the mortar's cavernous center for a more concentrated beating. If you don't have a mortar and pestle, continue to grind the paste to a finer texture in the food processor.

3 Transfer this to a small bowl and stir in the shrimp (or soybean) paste and the ground spices. For all this mellow work you will be gifted with a reddish-brown paste redolent of chilies and fruity aromas. Store it in a lidded glass jar in the refrigerator for up to a week or freeze it for up to three months.

Green Curry Paste

Makes ½ cup

¼ cup firmly packed fresh cilantro leaves

3 small shallots (each the size of a walnut), coarsely chopped

8 to 10 fresh green Thai chilies, stems removed

1 stalk lemongrass (lower 3 inches), coarsely chopped (see Tips, page 56)

3 pieces (each the size of a quarter) fresh galangal (see Tips, page 48)

2 medium fresh lime leaves, middle rib stripped (see Tips, page 48)

1 tablespoon shrimp paste or brown soybean paste (see Tips, page 48)

1 Pile the cilantro, shallots, chilies, lemongrass, galangal, and lime leaves into the bowl of a food processor. Pulse the ingredients to a coarse paste. At this point I usually like to transfer the mixture to a mortar and pound it into a smoother paste with a pestle, using a spatula to contain it in the mortar's cavernous center for a more concentrated beating. If you don't have a mortar and pestle, continue to grind it to a finer texture in the food processor.

You may need to add 2 tablespoons water to it to fashion a smoother grind.

2 Transfer this to a small bowl and stir in the shrimp (or soybean) paste. For all this mellow work, you will be gifted with a greenish-brown paste redolent of chilies and fruity aromas. Store it in a lidded glass jar in the refrigerator for up to a week or freeze it for up to 3 months.

TIPS

✦ Fresh Thai red chilies are common in the produce section of large supermarkets and stores that stock produce used in many Asian countries. If unavailable, grab a bag of dried red chilies (like chile de arbol or bird's-eye chilies) and reconstitute the amount called for in the recipe under boiling hot water, about 30 minutes.

✦ Aji amarillo chiles, indigenous to Peru, are not the easiest to find in supermarkets in the United States. These orangish-yellow chiles are quite perfumy, with a heat level comparable to that of a serrano chile. These are available in stores that stock Latin American produce and groceries. A more convenient form is a jar of aji amarillo paste that you can refrigerate for a month or freeze for up to six months.

✦ Fresh galangal, ginger, and turmeric are close siblings from the same family of rhizomes. Galangal and ginger are very common in Southeast Asian markets, while turmeric, even though found in the same stores, is seasonal. Galangal is very menthol-like in aroma and much harder to slice through. Get the pieces that are firm to the touch with a clean, dry surface. If you don't plan to use all of them in a recipe, slice and freeze them in ziptop bags. You don't even need to thaw them when using them to make your next batch of curry paste. And no, you do not need to peel the skin before use. If certain ends of the rhizome appear dry or even moldy, slice that end off before use. The gut of that rhizome will still be smooth and perfumed.

✦ I love the look of lime leaves, as they seem so perfectly dark green, glistening, and almost leathery with a slightly woody rib. It is best to slice them along the midrib and discard it before use. A few leaves go a long way and they have a relatively long life, given the fact they store well in the freezer. Most common in the produce section of Southeast Asian stores, they are called makrut in Thailand.

✦ Shrimp paste is made from dried, salted, and fermented shrimp. It tastes nothing like it smells (which can be off-putting to some) when you cook it in a curry. It imbues an essential umami taste and provides that je ne sais quoi to every recipe that includes it. If you are a vegetarian, I have given you the option of using a brown soybean paste (made with salted and fermented soybeans) that is a perfect stand-in for the shrimp paste.

Yellow Curry Paste

Makes 1 cup

1 tablespoon coriander seeds

3 small (each the size of a walnut) shallots, coarsely chopped

3 or 4 large cloves garlic

3 to 5 fresh or frozen yellow aji amarillo chiles or 1 tablespoon aji amarillo chile paste (see Tips, page 48)

2 stalks lemongrass (lower 3 inches), coarsely chopped (see Tips, page 56)

3 pieces (each the size of a quarter) fresh galangal (see Tips, page 48)

3 pieces (each the size of a quarter) fresh ginger

4 pieces (each the size of a dime) fresh turmeric, or 1 teaspoon ground turmeric

3 medium fresh lime leaves, middle rib stripped (see Tips, page 48)

1 tablespoon shrimp paste or brown soybean paste (see Tips, page 48)

1 Preheat a small skillet over medium-high heat. Once the pan is at the right temperature (usually takes 2 to 3 minutes), sprinkle in the coriander. Shake the skillet or use a spoon to stir the seeds around frequently until they turn an even reddish-brown color with a scintillating, citrus-like aroma, 1 to 2 minutes. Transfer them to a small bowl or plate to cool. Once cool to the touch, transfer them to a spice grinder (or clean coffee grinder) and pulverize them until they have the texture of finely ground black pepper.

2 Meanwhile, pour about ½ cup water into a blender jar and pile in the shallots, garlic, aji chiles or paste, lemongrass, galangal, ginger, turmeric, lime leaves, and shrimp or soybean paste along with the ground coriander. Puree the ingredients, scraping the inside of the jar as needed to contain them all in one focused pile for a smooth puree. Yes, when you open the lid, you will utter the word "wowee," I promise. Store it in a glass jar for a week to ten days in the refrigerator or the freezer for up to a month.

THE THAI VEGETARIAN

With the influence of Buddhism and the Buddhist monks in Thailand, who were masters at crafting meat analogues (I have a marvelous memory of eating at a vegetarian restaurant with a strong Buddhist influence in New York called the Zen Palate in the 1990s with the late Florence Lin, the grande dame of Chinese cooking), tofu arrived in Thailand in all its versatile glory. This particular curry uses an extra-firm tofu, pressed and pan-fried, to give you that same textural complexity of poultry (yes, everything tastes like chicken!). The flavors in this are reflective of a southern (Thai, that is) curry, the rich coconut milk providing an essential backdrop to the potent red chiles in the paste.

Pan-Fried Tofu with Red Curry Paste

Têāhû p̣hạd phrik p̄heā •→• Serves 4

2 tablespoons canola oil

1 pound extra-firm tofu, drained, pressed, and cut into 1-inch cubes (see Tips)

2 tablespoons Red Curry Paste (page 46)

4 small (each roughly the size of a golf ball) baby green eggplants, stemmed and quartered (see Tips)

1 medium red or white potato, peeled and cut into 1-inch cubes

1 small red bell pepper, stemmed, seeded, and cut into 1-inch cubes

½ cup sliced bamboo shoots (drained if using canned)

1 can (14 ounces) unsweetened coconut milk

2 tablespoons fish or soy sauce

2 tablespoons finely chopped fresh Thai or sweet basil (see Tips)

3 cups cooked jasmine rice (see Tips)

1 Heat the oil in a Dutch oven or large saucepan over medium heat. Once the oil appears to shimmer, add the tofu cubes and stir-fry them until they turn light brown along the sides. Transfer them onto a plate.

2 To the same oil, carefully add the curry paste, stir-frying the potent mélange, as the chilies within elevate their capsaicin heat and send you into a throat-clearing moment, 1 to 2 minutes. Yes, adequate venting or opening a window is fair game.

3 Add the eggplants, potato, bell pepper, and bamboo shoots to the pan. Shake the coconut milk well, pour it over the vegetables, and scrape the pan to release any collected bits of spices, chili paste, and other ingredients, thus effectively deglazing the pan.

4 Add the tofu and fish sauce and bring the curry to a boil. Cover the pan, stirring occasionally, to allow the potatoes and eggplant to become fork-tender, 10 to 12 minutes. During the last few minutes of cooking, remove the lid and continue to simmer uncovered to allow the sauce to thicken a bit.

5 Serve sprinkled with the basil alongside a bowl of jasmine rice.

TIPS

✦ To press the tofu, drain it and place it on a cutting board or plate between paper towels. Press down firmly with your hand to get rid of the excess moisture.

✦ Eggplant, part of the nightshade group (think potatoes and chilies), was introduced to North America in the early sixteenth century. The earlier cultivars were small and round (hence the "egg" in eggplant). With over sixty varieties of eggplant found here, the variety most revered in Thailand is one called Kermit (named after the lovable green Muppet) in North America. The Thai variety, like the American one, has a thick skin with a very subtle hint of bitter but is sweeter and creamier when cooked. Elizabeth Schneider, in her groundbreaking 2001 book *Vegetables from Amaranth to Zucchini*, so aptly describes the texture and look of cooked eggplant: "Cooking changes the hues and forms drastically, from a glowing garden of Eden to a compost heap." I have primarily seen this variety of eggplant in Southeast Asian supermarkets and farmers' markets. Yes, you can use any variety that is easily accessible to you, should you not have any inclination to try this particular kind.

✦ Sweet basil is pervasive. Thai basil is harder to find but generally available at Southeast Asian markets. Peppery, with an anise-like flavor, it adds an extra layer of refinement to this curry. (You may also see Thai holy basil sold, but note that the two herbs are actually different species with different flavor profiles. Among Hindus—as evidence of the deep influence of the religion in Thailand—it is common to find a Thai holy basil plant in almost every courtyard or balcony.)

✦ The call for coming to the table in Thailand translates to "let's eat rice." So it is no wonder that Thailand grows and cultivates a perfumed variety called jasmine, after its namesake flower. Long-grained and not so starchy as the more mundane varieties, it is easy to find in just about every grocery store. A cup of uncooked rice yields about 3 cups cooked. See page 193 on how to cook the perfect grain of rice.

L'INDOCHINE FRANÇAISE

The French occupied Vietnam between 1858 and 1954, weaving their gustatory influences into Vietnamese cooking through their European techniques and ingredients. Baguettes and many things French influenced Vietnam's signature sandwich, the banh mi, while curry powders brought in a taste of the exotic from France's occupation of Pondicherry in southeastern India. Northern Vietnam leaned toward Chinese fixings and methods, while the southern region of Vietnam fell in love with the world of coconut milks and curry powders.

This chicken curry comes to me via my close friend and colleague Andrea Nguyen, a renowned, award-winning cookbook author and teacher, whom I have known for more than fifteen years. She was generous enough to share with me her childhood favorite from her book *Into the Vietnamese Kitchen*, which I have adapted. Nguyen promises a curry with big flavors, thanks to lots of lemongrass, curry powder, and ginger. The coconut milk cloaks the chicken with creaminess. Serve it alongside a French baguette, rice, or noodles.

TIPS

✦ Stalks of lemongrass are now common at many supermarkets, as well as farmers' markets and Southeast Asian grocery stores. They are easy to prep. Slice off the root end of the stalk (about 3 inches) and cut it in half lengthwise. Cut each half into thin strips. Stack them up and cut them into desired pieces. (One stalk will yield 1 generous tablespoon finely chopped; a coarse chop will yield a greater volume.)

✦ The flavors in my Madras curry powder reflect the tastes of the southern region of India, part of which—like Vietnam—was occupied by the French. It works perfectly in this dish, but feel free to use Vietnamese curry powder if you can find it.

✦ Removing the skin from cut-up poultry is a cinch. Lay the pieces on a cutting board, and using paper towels to improve your grip, pull apart the skin.

✦ Keep the chopped potatoes submerged in a bowl of water. Drain and pat dry just before use.

Chicken Lemongrass Curry with Potatoes

Cà-ri gà ⚬ Serves 4

3 stalks lemongrass (lower 3 inches of each), coarsely chopped (see Tips)

3 pieces (each the size of a quarter) fresh ginger

1 medium yellow onion, coarsely chopped

2 tablespoons canola oil

2 tablespoons Madras Curry Powder (page 19; see Tips)

¼ teaspoon ground red pepper (cayenne)

2½ pounds bone-in chicken thighs or drumsticks, skin removed (see Tips)

1 can (about 14 ounces) unsweetened coconut milk

1½ teaspoons coarse sea salt

½ teaspoon coarsely cracked black peppercorns

1 pound red potatoes, peeled, and cut into 1-inch chunks (see Tips)

2 tablespoons coarsely chopped fresh cilantro

1 large lime, cut into wedges

1 Pile the lemongrass, ginger, and onion into a food processor bowl. Pulverize the aromatic yet pungent ingredients to a well-minced blend.

2 Heat the oil in a large skillet or a Dutch oven over medium-high heat. Once the oil appears to shimmer, scrape the food processor's aromatic contents into the oil and stir-fry the medley until light brown around the edges and fragrant, 2 to 3 minutes.

3 Sprinkle in the curry powder and the ground red pepper and stir them in. The heat in the lemongrass sauté will be just right to cook the spices without burning them, 15 seconds.

4 Add the chicken pieces to the pan, giving it all a good stir to coat them with the spiced curry base, 1 to 2 minutes.

5 Shake the coconut milk well and add it to the pan along with the salt and pepper. Scrape the bottom of the pan to release all the browned bits of goodness back into the sauce, effectively deglazing the pan. As the curry comes to a boil, lower the heat to medium and simmer the contents, covered, stirring occasionally until the chicken is partially cooked (still very pink in the middle), about 15 minutes. Add the potatoes and continue to simmer, covered, stirring occasionally, until the potatoes are fork-tender, and the chicken, when pierced in the thickest part of the meat, releases clear juices, 10 to 12 minutes.

6 Serve the curry sprinkled with the cilantro and pass around the wedges of limes for an individual spritz of sourness.

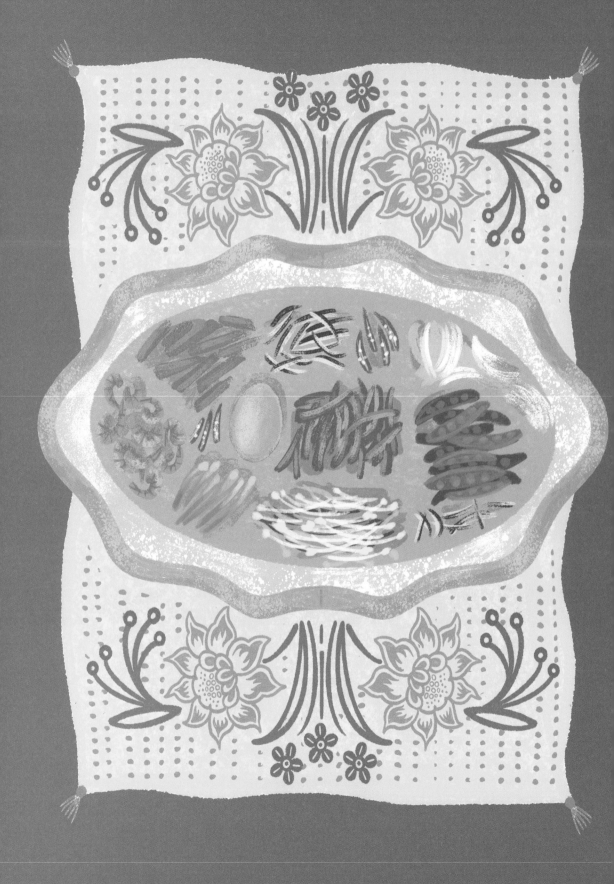

A TASTE OF MALAYSIA

With the distinction of being the only place in the world that is an island, a nation, and a city, the Republic of Singapore rests just off the southern tip of peninsular Malaysia and harbors a cuisine unlike others, drawing from a wide variety of influences—the Malays, Chinese, Indians, the English (who were there as the East India Trading Company in 1819), Portuguese, Indonesians, Thai, Japanese, and Korean, among others. Chinese immigration in the 1820s and 1840s, primarily to work the tin mines in Singapore, was significant; these days the majority of residents in Singapore are of Chinese descent.

Which brings me to these curried noodles. They are not native to Singapore—which has its own curried noodle dishes, such as the Nonya broth known as laksa—but were created in the pans of a Hong Kong chef and are a steadfast favorite in the Chinese restaurants in North America and Europe that dish up Cantonese treasures. Curry powder, specifically the Madras curry powder, is a reflection of its introduction by the Anglo-Indian traders; many a southern Chinese dish experienced a generous sprinkle or two of this predominantly turmeric-flavored blend. Similar to a Malaysian noodle dish called Xin Zhou Mee Fen, these rice vermicelli noodles combine with seafood (and often meats like chicken and pork) and green vegetables. My friend Girija Padmanabhan (see page 64), with roots in Malaysia via Kerala, India, reminisces about this comfort food and includes only green Chinese vegetables like choy sum and bok choy (both members of the Brassica family—think mustard, cabbage, cauliflower), bean sprouts, and scallions. I like to eat the rainbow and so have taken the liberty of including carrots and red bell peppers in my version. Whichever your fancy, the dish is addictive.

Curry Noodles with Shrimp

Mee kari dengan udang ⋅•⋅ Serves 4

6 ounces dried rice sticks (rice vermicelli)

Boiling water

1 tablespoon Madras Curry Powder (page 19; see Note)

5 tablespoons canola oil

1 large egg, slightly beaten

1 medium yellow onion, cut in half and thinly sliced

1 large carrot, peeled, cut into 3-inch strips like matchsticks

1 small red bell pepper, cored, seeds removed, and cut into thin matchsticks

3 slices (each the thickness and size of a quarter) fresh ginger, cut crosswise into very thin matchsticks

2 fresh green Thai chilies, stems removed, cut into thin slices (do not discard the seeds)

10 small to medium snow pea pods, strings removed along each flat side

8 ounces shrimp (30–40 per pound), peeled, deveined, and tail off

1 ounce bean sprouts (not the alfalfa kind)

1 scallion, trimmed, cut into 3-inch strips (white bulb and green top)

2 tablespoons fish sauce

2 tablespoons soy sauce

1 tablespoon rice vinegar

½ teaspoon coarse sea salt

½ teaspoon unrefined sugar

2 tablespoons finely chopped fresh cilantro

1 Place the dried noodles in a large bowl or baking dish, preferably one that can hold the noodles as long as they are, that is, unbroken. Pour boiling water over the noodles to submerge them and allow them to soften (but not be mushy), 6 to 8 minutes. Immediately drain them in a colander and run cool water through them to take the edge off the heat so the noodles don't continue to cook. It's great if they remain lukewarm. Toss them with 1 teaspoon of the curry powder and set aside as you get the stir-fry ready.

2 Heat a tablespoon of the oil in a wok or a large frying pan over medium-high to almost high heat. Once the oil appears to shimmer, pour the beaten egg into it. It will immediately expand and cook, turning into a sunny brown disposition, about 1 minute. Scoop it out onto a plate. Cut it into thin strips.

3 Now drizzle 2 tablespoons of the oil into the same wok, which will heat the oil immediately to the right temperature. Add the onion and carrot and stir-fry vigorously for a minute or two to slightly cook them. Add the pepper, ginger, chilies, and pea pods and continue to stir-fry another minute or two. Sprinkle another teaspoon of the curry powder over the crisp vegetables. A quick stir will ensure an even coating, and the heat will be just right to cook the spice blend without burning it. Remove the yellowed vegetables to the plate with the egg strips.

4 Back to the hot wok, now drizzle in another tablespoon of oil. Add the shrimp to the pan and stir-fry the shellfish for just a minute until they barely start to curl. Mix in the final teaspoon of the curry powder. Remove from the pan and add them to the growing pile of vegetables and eggs.

5 Drizzle the final tablespoon of the oil into the wok. Grab handfuls of the seasoned rice noodles and toss them in the pan to allow the noodles to rewarm and to cook the spices in the curry powder, 1 to 2 minutes.

6 Now pile in all the set-aside shrimp, vegetables, and eggs, along with the sprouts, scallion, fish sauce, soy sauce, rice vinegar, salt, and sugar. Give it all a good mix and serve immediately, sprinkled with the cilantro.

✦ *The curry powder you see in the recipe may seem a lot, but trust me, I know what I am doing (for the most part!). I sprinkle that in batches onto the various components in the dish (noodles, shrimp, vegetables) to fashion a complex and layered flavor to the tender, cooked-just-right rice vermicelli noodles. Each mouthful heightens the addiction.*

VARIATION

Adapt your vegetables based on what you feel like eating. Try the all-green vegetable combination of choy sum, bok choy, spinach, Chinese broccoli, and scallions for an equally satisfying experience.

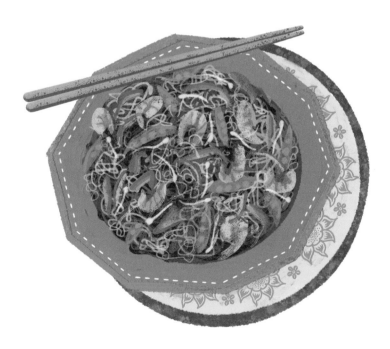

NONYA COMFORT

Malaysia has been a meeting point of cultures for centuries and centuries because of its location at the crossroads of ancient and modern trading routes that included Buddhists and Indians. As is true in many parts of the world, food, and in particular spices, has always been a "weapon" used to control a civilization's resources—and Malaysia was no exception. The Indian traders monopolized the spice trade while positioned in Java and nurtured more rice cultivation around 1000 CE (the grain became a staple after the Buddhists introduced it to the region as early as 300 CE). Rice, mangoes, eggplant, onions, cumin, and coriander became major players in Malaysian curries as a result—and with plenty of access to edible treasures from the sea, it is no wonder that Malaysian cooking now cannot live without the marriage of seafood curries and rice.

When the British East India Company took control of the island of Penang in 1786, they eventually ousted the Dutch colonizers (who were only briefly in place as seemed to be the pattern in this colonization "game") with the help of the local sultans, and brought what is now Malaysia under their complete power. The next 200 years saw a large migration of poor Chinese workers from southern China and indentured labor from Tamil-speaking southern India to work the rubber and palm plantations. This mélange of cultures morphed into a cuisine that included influences not only from the Chinese and Indian, but also from the Dutch, Portuguese, and English. An alliance of Chinese men (called babas) and Chinese-Malaysian women (called Nonya or Nyonya) gave birth to the Nonya or Peranakan cuisine that combined Chinese techniques with local ingredients like tamarind, lemongrass, lime leaves, coconut milk, and galangal.

The most popular of the curries in this Nonya cuisine is kari ayam, a bone-in chicken stew scented with spices like star anise, turmeric, cinnamon, and cumin. Curry pastes, similar to those found in Thailand, cloak the meat, as coconut milk sweetens the presence of chilies and other assertive ingredients. Serve this perfumed curry with the flaky flatbread Roti Canai (page 65), a perfect eating tool to mop up all that succulent sauce.

Chicken Curry
with Lemongrass and Curry Leaves

Kari ayam ⦾ Serves 4

FOR THE CURRY PASTE

1 tablespoon Malaysian curry powder (see Tips)

6 pieces (each the size of a quarter) fresh ginger

2 pieces (each the size of a quarter) fresh galangal

1 stalk lemongrass (lower 3 inches), coarsely chopped

4 fresh red bird's-eye (Thai) chilies, stemmed

2 large shallots, coarsely chopped

FOR THE CHICKEN CURRY

2 tablespoons canola oil

1 teaspoon cumin seeds

2 sticks (about 3 inches each) cinnamon

2 star anise

2 pounds bone-in chicken thighs or drumsticks, skin removed

1 pound red potatoes, peeled, and cut into 2-inch pieces (see Tips)

1 can (about 14 ounces) unsweetened coconut milk

15 to 20 medium to large fresh curry leaves (see page 33)

1 stalk lemongrass (lower 3 inches), cut in half lengthwise

1 teaspoon coarse sea salt

2 tablespoons fish sauce

2 tablespoons finely chopped fresh cilantro

1 Start by making the curry paste. Pour ½ cup water into a blender jar and plunk in the curry powder, ginger, galangal, lemongrass, chilies, and shallots. Puree the mélange to a smooth paste, scraping the inside of the jar as needed to contain the paste and enable an even pulverization. Scrape this light orange-red paste, with a strong fruity aroma, into a bowl.

2 To make the curry, heat the oil over medium-high heat in a Dutch oven or a large saucepan. Once the oil appears to shimmer, sprinkle in the cumin, cinnamon, and star anise. They will instantly start to sizzle and scent the oil (not to mention the kitchen), 5 to 10 seconds.

3 Carefully lay the chicken pieces in a single layer in the pan, allowing the meat to sear, covered, now on medium heat, flipping the pieces over halfway through, until sunny brown, dotting its meaty landscape with the cumin seeds, 5 to 7 minutes. Remove the chicken from the pan and set it on a plate.

4 In that same oil, add the potatoes and sear them, covered as well, stirring them around occasionally, to ensure an even browning, 3 to 5 minutes. Carefully add ¼ cup of the curry paste, coating the potatoes with its orange-red complexion, creating that back-of-the-throat burn and cough from the capsaicin in the puree. Cover the pan to contain the splattering, and continue to cook the paste, stirring carefully and occasionally, until its color changes to an intense reddish-brown, 3 to 5 minutes.

(recipe continues)

5 Shake the coconut milk well and pour it in. It will almost instantly start to boil, thanks to the pan's heat. Scrape the bottom of the pan to release all those collected bits of spice and flavor, scenting the sauce with a light orange-colored floral bouquet. Stir in the curry leaves, lemongrass, salt, the chicken pieces including any pooled liquid on the plate, and the fish sauce.

6 Reduce the heat to medium-low and continue to briskly simmer the curry, covered, stirring occasionally, until the potatoes are fork-tender and the chicken pieces when pierced with a fork release a clear liquid, 20 to 25 minutes.

7 Serve sprinkled with the cilantro.

VARIATION

Make it vegetarian (and in this case vegan as well) by eliminating the chicken. Instead, use about 10 ounces of unripe jackfruit (some health food stores now carry them in the freezer). Any Southeast Asian or South Asian grocery store, and possibly your neighborhood Trader Joe's, also sells them canned. Drain the brine before use. If you are lucky enough to find the fresh variety, savor those chunks. They will take a bit longer to become tender. For a meatier texture, I always pan-fry the fresh chunks before use. And you may pan-fry them the same way you sear the chicken in the recipe. Otherwise almost everything else remains the same—make sure to eliminate the fish sauce in the recipe and use a dark soy sauce instead.

TIPS

✦ You can procure a Malaysian brand of curry powder online or at any Southeast Asian supermarket that carries groceries from Malaysia. Or make your own at home (cheaper and far more flavorful, if I may say so!). Measure out the following spices into a spice grinder (or clean coffee grinder):

1 tablespoon coriander seeds

2 teaspoons cumin seeds

½ teaspoon whole cloves

½ teaspoon black peppercorns

½ teaspoon fennel seeds

Seeds from 4 to 6 green or white cardamom pods

4 to 6 dried red cayenne chiles (or chile de arbol), stems discarded

2 star anise

1 stick (about 3 inches long) cinnamon, broken up

Pulverize to a fine powder. Tap the lid to release any of the intoxicating blend back into the grinder's cavity. Transfer this to a small bowl and stir in 1 tablespoon ground turmeric. Store in a tight-lidded container outside the refrigerator in a cool, dry spot in your pantry away from sunlight.

✦ Keep the chopped potatoes submerged in a bowl of water. Drain and pat dry just before use.

A MALAYSIAN STAPLE

My friend the gorgeously intelligent Girija Padmanabhan loves to replicate flavors from her childhood home in Malaysia. Born in Singapore in 1965 to parents from the southwestern state of Kerala, she moved with them to Malaysia soon afterward, to the city of Ipoh, a smaller Chinese immigrant community of tin miners, just north of Kuala Lumpur. Fluent in Cantonese, she grew up savoring Chinese, Indian, and Malay foods. After graduation and marriage, she migrated to the United States for better opportunities, adopting the flavors of her new homeland, yet hanging on to the foods of her childhood.

The street foods in Malaysia were diverse, reflecting the tastes of many of its immigrants. She confesses to a penchant for buying roti canai (pronounced *cha-nai*): thin, flaky, and rich flatbreads to wrap around curries with legumes and those with seafoods and meats swimming in a broth of shrimp and chicken scented with red chilies, ginger, shallots, galangal, and a Malaysian curry powder. "We never made roti canai at home," she muses, as her family bought them from a Muslim Indian vendor (with shared roots in Kerala) at a cost of a few pennies. His rotis were pan-fried in a sea of oil, and he topped them with an egg, shallots, and a sprinkle of cayenne.

I remembered my experience with these breads the first time I visited Kerala, where I watched a street vendor making them, mesmerized by his speedy technique, as he shaped the dough by hand and rolled it into a coil. He then rerolled it into a circle, slapped it paper-thin onto a hot griddle to let it brown on both sides, and then slathered it with liberal amounts of ghee. A corner of his flat griddle held two large pots of curries, one vegetarian and the other a chicken curry. Both were coconut milk–based, redolent of spices from the Malabar Coast: green cardamom, hand-crushed black Tellicherry peppercorns, and thin furls of cinnamon bark, similar to the flavors that punctuated curries in Malaysia as well. Here is my version, sans egg or vast amounts of oil, yet still addictive, flaky, thin, and rich.

Flaky Griddle-Cooked Breads

Roti canai ⟶ Makes 6 rotis

3 cups unbleached all-purpose flour, plus extra for dusting

2 teaspoons baking powder

1 teaspoon coarse sea salt

2 tablespoons ghee (for homemade, see Variation, page 95) or melted butter, plus extra for brushing

½ cup buttermilk, at room temperature

¼ cup sweetened condensed milk

½ to ¾ cup hot tap water

Maldon sea salt for sprinkling (or something comparable)

1 Thoroughly combine the flour, baking powder, and salt in a large bowl. Drizzle the 2 tablespoons ghee over the flour mixture, rubbing the flour between your palms and fingers to evenly distribute the ghee.

2 Pour the buttermilk and condensed milk over the flour mixture and quickly stir it in. The flour will still be very dry, with a few wet spots.

3 Pour a few tablespoons of the hot tap water over the flour, stirring it in as you do so. Repeat until the flour comes together to form a soft ball. Using your hands (as long as they're clean, I think they're the best tool), gather the

ball, picking up any dry flour (wet hands do help with this) in the bottom of the bowl, and knead it to form a smooth, soft ball of dough (do this in the bowl or on a lightly floured surface). If it's a little too wet, dust it with a little flour, kneading it in after every dusting until you get the right soft, dry consistency. (If you used your hands to make the dough from the start, they will be caked with clumps of dough. Scrape them back into the bowl. Wash and dry your hands thoroughly and return to the dough to knead it. You will get a much better feel for the dough's consistency with dry hands.) The dough has to be super soft but not sticky.

4 Cover the dough with plastic wrap or a slightly dampened cloth, and let it rest at room temperature for about 30 minutes.

5 Using your hands, shape the dough into an 18-inch log (lightly flour the work surface if necessary). Cut it crosswise into 6 pieces and shape each piece into a ball. Press each ball flat to form a patty. Brush them with ghee. Cover the patties with plastic wrap to let the gluten in them soften, about 15 minutes.

(recipe continues)

6 Brush a part of the countertop or a clean cutting board with ghee. Place a round on it and roll it as thin as you can without tearing the dough. Don't worry about its shape. Brush the top liberally with ghee. Lift the edge closest to you and roll the dough into a tight cigar-shaped log. Form the log into a tight coil, tucking and pressing the end under the coil. Then flatten the coil to form a patty. Repeat with the remaining dough and keep the patties under wrap for another 15 minutes or so.

7 Tear off a large sheet of aluminum foil, fold it in half lengthwise, and set it aside. Place the ghee near the stove, with a pastry brush handy.

8 Heat a medium skillet (preferably nonstick or cast iron) over medium heat.

9 While the skillet is heating, lightly flour a small work area (I put flour in a sugar shaker so it's a light dusting) near the stove and place a dough patty on it (leave the others under cover). Roll it out to form a round roughly 7 to 9 inches in diameter, dusting it with flour as needed. Make sure the round is evenly thin, with no tears on the surface.

10 Lift the round and plop it into the hot skillet. Cook until the surface has some bumps and bubbles, and the underside has some brown spots and looks cooked, 3 to 4 minutes. Immediately flip it over and cook until the other side has brown spots, 3 to 4 minutes.

11 Brush the round with ghee and flip it over to sear it, about 30 seconds. Brush the top with ghee and flip it over to sear it as well, about 30 seconds. Sprinkle a bit of the Maldon salt on one side. Slip the roti between the layers of foil to keep it warm.

12 Repeat with the remaining dough, stacking the finished rotis under the foil.

13 Serve immediately.

✦ *These breads (cooked) do freeze very well. Wrap them in aluminum foil, separating with pieces of wax or parchment paper, and place in a freezer-safe ziptop bag. They will keep for 6 months. When ready for using, bring them to room temperature to thaw. Reheat in a preheated skillet, over medium heat, until warmed through, 2 to 4 minutes.*

CURRY TIFFIN

Even though Chinese merchants had had well established trading relationships in North Borneo for centuries, Britain formally claimed the territory for its own in 1882. Laborers and farmers from China and India were enticed by the promise of agricultural work, and aided by official charter, to migrate to what became British North Borneo. The anglicized curries, which they brought with them, became a staple of the colonials' suppers; the phrase *curry tiffin* was coined to describe the assorted piles of "Bombay duck" (see Tips), coconut shreds, pineapple, dried fruits, nuts, and other small dishes that accompanied the yellow spiced stew, together yielding a goulash of tastes, textures, and colors that sated the colonials' palates.

My take on this codfish curry breaks it into distinct parts that, together, suggest the "anything and everything goes" approach of a traditional curry tiffin.

Pan-Fried Salted Cod Curry with Cucumber Relish

Bacalhau gulai ·•· Serves 4

1½ pounds skinless salt cod fillets or dried bombil ("Bombay duck"; see Tips)

2 tablespoons finely chopped fresh ginger

1 fresh green serrano chile, stem removed, finely chopped (do not discard the seeds)

1 teaspoon coarse sea salt

½ cup dried unsweetened shredded coconut

4 tablespoons canola oil

1 medium red onion, finely chopped

1 large tomato, cored and finely chopped

1 teaspoon tamarind paste or concentrate (see Tips, page 124)

2 teaspoons Madras Curry Powder (page 19)

¼ cup finely chopped fresh cilantro

½ cup Cream of Wheat (not instant) or fine dried breadcrumbs

FOR SERVING

1 small cucumber, peeled, seeded, and cut into ¼-inch cubes

2 tablespoons Major Grey's Mango Chutney (see Tips, page 170)

1 Soak the salt cod or bombil in water to cover for about 30 minutes to remove the excess salt. Discard the water and give the fish a good rinse. Pat it dry before using.

2 Combine the ginger, chile, and ½ teaspoon of the salt in a small bowl. Smear each side of the fish with this mixture. Refrigerate, covered, to allow the flavors to permeate the fish, 30 minutes to 1 hour.

3 Preheat a medium skillet over medium heat. Once the pan is hot, sprinkle in the shredded coconut and toast it, stirring almost constantly, until the shreds are reddish-brown and smell nutty, 2 to 3 minutes. Transfer them to a small bowl. Heat 2 tablespoons of the oil in the same skillet over medium heat. The oil will appear to shimmer almost instantly (as the pan is still hot from toasting the coconut). Add the

onion and stir-fry until it is soft and light brown around the edges with a light purple hue, about 10 minutes.

4 Stir in the tomato, tamarind paste, curry powder, and the remaining ½ teaspoon salt. Cook, uncovered, stirring occasionally, until the tomatoes soften but still appear firm, 5 to 10 minutes. Stir in the cilantro and the toasted coconut. Remove the skillet from the heat and cover the sauce to keep it warm.

5 Spread the Cream of Wheat on a plate. One by one, press the spice-coated fish fillets into the wheat, covering both sides with a gritty armor.

6 Heat the remaining 2 tablespoons oil in a large nonstick skillet over medium heat. Add the coated fish fillets and fry until they are crisp and brown on both sides, 4 to 8 minutes per side (depending on the thickness of the fish). The fish's interior should be barely starting to flake.

7 To serve the curry, place the fried fish on a platter and top with the tart-spicy, hot-sweet sauce.

8 Combine the cucumber and the chutney in a medium bowl. Serve this simple but complex-tasting compote alongside the fish curry.

TIPS

✦ A bowl of steamed rice is always a great accompaniment to the curry as it gives the eater a balanced backdrop for the robust flavors in the curry. Yes, as the British would choose, a few pints of a dark beer are great chasers to the meal.

✦ The lizardfish (*Harpadon nehereus*) is known as bombil in Marathi (the language of the state Maharashtra in India). It is the local favorite of the Koli fishing community native to the original seven islands that formed Bombay (now Mumbai). The fresh fish are considered ideal when small (6 to 8 inches), though they can sometimes reach 12 inches in length. When dried, bombil is nicknamed "Bombay duck," though it has nothing to do with the quacky bird. The phrase is said to be an adaptation of Bombay daak, the mail (daak) train that transported crates of dried fish to the eastern cities of India, a region notoriously passionate about fish in any size, shape, or form. The pungent aroma of the fish permeated the wooden boards of the train's compartments, much to the disgust of the British colonizers. But they soon took a liking to its umami goodness and began punctuating curries and rice with bits of roasted "Bombay duck," whose flavor is reminiscent of pickled herring.

THE SPICE ISLANDS

The sixteenth century exposed Indonesia, with its 13,000-plus islands, to European traders, who were intoxicated by the so-called Spice Islands, with their beguiling aromas and the promise of riches from their nutmeg, mace, ginger, turmeric, tamarind, and cloves. No wonder conquerors from China, Portugal, India, Holland, and Great Britain fought for control of the region— also known as the Banda Islands—over the centuries. Even though nutmeg and mace were *the* most lucrative commodity for traders, they never became important inclusions in the cuisine of Indonesia. The Dutch had control over the spices for 250 years and then the British for 14 years, during which time the spices were transported to and planted in Grenada, thereby diminishing the Bandas Islands' exclusivity as the source of mace and nutmeg.

Nancy Coune and her husband, Jody Sipe, friends and fellow Minnesotans, traveled to the Indonesian islands of Bali and Java multiple times during the 1980s and spent enough time there to become enamored of the country's culture, inhabitants, artifacts, shadow plays, dyed batik fabrics, and food. Nancy taught me about regional curries, condiments, and breads that reflected the influences of traders and settlers, similar to what is found in Malaysia, Thailand, India, China, and Holland. Indonesia's curry pastes, like those of Thailand, are a mosaic of spices, flavorings, and herbs, weaving in that quintessential balance of complexity. Gulais and opors (coconut milk curries), sotos (soups), sayurs (thin-bodied, vegetable-rich stews), rendangs (dry, as in sauceless, beef and water buffalo curry), and karis (coconut milk stews reflecting the Dutch–Indonesian alliance) are some of the offerings from different parts of this widespread archipelago.

Gulais from Sumatra, Java, Borneo, and the Malay peninsula—replete with turmeric, spices, herbs, meats, seafood, and vegetables—are perhaps the most iconic of the curries. Characteristic of Minangkabau cuisine from western Sumatra, gulai curry is offered at many a Padang restaurant. My version here is adapted from one of Nancy and Jody's recipes. It captures the essence of that Indian-influenced Indonesian curry, and as always, I serve it alongside steeped white rice (see page 193) to mop up all those rich flavors in the sauce.

Unripe Jackfruit and Potatoes with Mussels

Gulai cubadak ⋅→⋅ Serves 6

Canola oil for deep-frying

1 can (20 ounces) young, unripe jackfruit, drained and cut into 1-inch pieces (see Tips, and also page 62)

1 large russet potato, peeled and cut into 1-inch pieces (see Tips)

2 pounds mussels, in the shells

1 cup coconut water

1 can (about 14 ounces) unsweetened coconut milk

2 tablespoons Yellow Curry Paste (see page 50)

½ teaspoon freshly grated nutmeg (see Tips)

¼ cup roasted candlenuts or roasted macadamia nuts, ground (see Tips)

1 teaspoon unrefined cane sugar

1 teaspoon coarse sea salt

4 pieces (each approximately 2 inches long and 1 inch wide) dried black mangosteen slices or 1 teaspoon tamarind paste (see Tips)

1 scallion, trimmed, white bulb and green top thinly sliced

1 Pour enough oil (2 to 3 inches deep) into a wok, Dutch oven, or medium saucepan. Heat the oil over medium to medium-high heat until a candy or oil thermometer inserted into the oil (without touching the pan's bottom) registers 350°F. An alternate way to see if the oil is at the right temperature for deep-frying is to stick a wooden skewer in the oil's center. If pearl-like bubbles form around the skewer's base, the oil is ready.

2 Line a plate or sheet pan with 3 or 4 sheets of paper towel. Once the oil is ready, gently plunk in the jackfruit pieces (I use a slotted spoon, fill it with the pieces, and submerge it in the oil). Stand back a little as the oil will splatter and bubble, but then subside to a gentle fry. Cook until the pieces turn light honey-brown and crispy, about 5 minutes. Remove them with the slotted spoon and allow them to drain on the paper towels to absorb excess grease.

3 Now add the potato pieces to the oil and allow them to lightly brown on the surface, 3 to 5 minutes. They will still be a bit firm and uncooked in the center. Add them to the jackfruit on the plate.

4 Pile the mussels into a large bowl. Quickly go through them and discard any broken or cracked shells. Scrub each mussel (although the ones available at any supermarket are actually quite clean) and remove the beards (2 or 3 strands dangling from one end of the shell—rather like a straggly goatee). Tap the shell if it's slightly ajar. If it closes shut, the mussel is alive and usable. If it does not shut, discard it, since this means it is dead. Plunk the prepared mussels into a colander and give them a good rinse.

5 Bring the coconut water to a boil in a Dutch oven or large saucepan over high heat. Add the mussels and cover the pot.

(recipe continues)

Cook, shaking the pot occasionally so they cook evenly, until they all open up to reveal plump, off-white meat, about 5 minutes. Discard any mussels that remain shut. Fish the mussels out of the water and transfer them to a plate. Pour the mussels-flavored coconut water into a measuring cup (in case you need to thin out the curry later).

6 To make the gulai, shake the coconut milk well and pour it into the same Dutch oven. Whisk in the curry paste, nutmeg, candlenuts, sugar, salt, and the dried mangosteen (or tamarind). Bring the mixture to a boil over medium heat, uncovered.

7 Pile in the fried jackfruit and potatoes and give it all a good stir. Place a lid on the pan and continue to simmer the curry vigorously, stirring occasionally, until the potatoes are tender, 5 to 8 minutes.

8 Add the mussels to the gulai and allow them to rewarm, 1 to 2 minutes. If the curry is too thick, add some of the reserved coconut water to thin it out.

9 Fish out the mangosteen slices and serve warm with the sliced scallion sprinkled on top.

TIPS

✦ Considered the largest fruit in the world (and found in tropical climates, including Indonesia where it is called nangka), jackfruits are heavy with a spiky skin. I always say it's best to leave it to the experts to cut the fruit up (which is quite sappy-sticky on the inside and requires super sharp knives and oil to separate the ripe yellow fruit meat with a strong musky smell from the off-white unripe portion). The yellow-fleshed ripe fruit houses a nut that is similar to a chestnut when roasted or cooked in stews. When unripe, the starchy flesh (yes, it is a sibling to breadfruit) is used in savory curries and has a meat-like texture, especially when fried. Now considered a "hip" alternative to meats in North America, this has been fashionable in other parts of the world for thousands of years. If you can't find it canned, use frozen: Thaw it, pat it dry between paper towels, and cut it into 1-inch cubes.

✦ Keep the chopped potatoes submerged in a bowl of water. Drain and pat dry just before use.

✦ I can't talk about Indonesia without mentioning its indigenous fruit-bearing nutmeg tree. The firm, light green, pear-shaped fruit has not one, but two aromatic spices. When you crack it open, you immediately see a weblike lacy covering with an orangish-brown (sometimes red) color around a dark brown shell. Carefully prying apart this web yields mace. Break open the shell and inside is the light brown nut commonly referred to as nutmeg. As with any spice, grind them fresh before use if the recipe calls for the ground version. In nutmeg's case, you grate it against the finer holes of a grater or use a specialized nutmeg grater. Intoxicating!

✦ Candlenuts (so named because their oil was used to make candles), very much macadamia-like in appearance (hence the alternative recommendation), are found in Indonesia, India, Thailand, and Malaysia. Roasted prior to use (because of toxic oils present), their flavor is mellow; when ground to the texture of coarse breadcrumbs, they provide body to the gulais in Indonesia. Cashews or even walnuts are okay options as well. And yes, if you have nut allergies, leave them out of the recipe.

✦ Mangosteen is known as kokum in India; in Indonesia it is called buah manggis. I've had plenty of luck finding the dried sections of mangosteen in Indian supermarkets. The fresh fruit is a product of the evergreen tree that bears ornamental-worthy pink flowers. The fruit itself is dark purple and has six to eight sections with seeds. Sour with a pleasant sweetness when ripe, these are used in gulais for that particular sweet-sour taste element. If unavailable, try sour tamarind paste (more commonly available in well-stocked grocery outlets).

CHINA: A RICE CULTURE

Chinese Buddhist monks traveled to India to study Buddhism and its related monastic values, rules, food habits, and ingredients around the third century CE. China had already begun farming rice in its southern regions by the Yangtze River around 6000 BCE. By the seventh century CE, Buddhist monasteries colonized parts of Southeast Asia and introduced rice irrigation there. The cultivation of a tougher, chewier variety of rice from Vietnam, called Champa, took hold due to a mandate from the government; higher qualities of white rice were reserved for the wealthy, with an occasional appearance at the peasant's table. Rice has always made its presence known around most of China, except the north, where millet and sorghum were easier to grow because of its drier conditions.

In a food culture like China's, nothing is wasted, and so leftover rice was always recycled in innovative ways. Bits of vegetables, meats, and eggs shored up the cooked rice while seasonings enlivened its flavors. Once the British had introduced Madras curry powder to China, it became an exotic addition to fried rice, providing subtle tastes, color, and aroma. I have sampled many a version in numerous restaurants that feature Cantonese cooking, but I always order it without the egg (a personal dietary choice). So here I share with you my eggless version (but I have given you the choice and have explained how to add it in the variation opposite), replete with all the requirements for comfort in a bowl.

TIP

✦ The key to a perfect fried rice is, of course, the rice. I always subject leftover rice to stir-frying with various ingredients and seasoning combinations, depending on my mood. It's a blank canvas for anything and everything, but it ultimately is all about using previously cooked rice that has been chilled. Even if your rice is of a starchy variety, chilling it will cool the starch and prevent the rice from being gummy so it will separate into single grains when broken up when clumped.

Wok-Seared Curried Fried Rice

Gali fen ch'ao fan ⋅→⋅ Serves 6

2 tablespoons canola oil

1 tablespoon finely chopped fresh ginger

2 large scallions, trimmed, white bulbs and green tops thinly sliced (keep them separate)

½ cup shredded cabbage

½ cup fresh or frozen sweet corn kernels

½ cup frozen green peas

¼ cup thinly sliced green or yellow beans

1 large carrot, peeled, trimmed, and thinly sliced into coins

1 serrano chile, stem discarded, finely chopped (do not discard the seeds)

3 cups cooked and cooled long-grain white rice (see Tip)

2 teaspoons Madras Curry Powder (page 19)

½ teaspoon coarse sea salt

¼ cup soy sauce

2 tablespoons Chinese rice wine vinegar

1 teaspoon toasted sesame oil

2 tablespoons finely chopped fresh cilantro

1 Preheat a wok or large skillet over medium-high heat. Add the oil, which should shimmer immediately in the hot pan. Add the ginger and the sliced white scallion bulb. Stir-fry the two until the ginger is light brown and fragrant, about 1 minute.

2 Toss in the cabbage, corn, peas, beans, carrot, and chile. Continue stir-frying the medley to cook the vegetables until they are crisp-tender, 3 to 5 minutes.

3 Add the cooled rice (if it is in lumps, break them up to separate the grains) along with the curry powder and salt. Once the rice starts to warm up, the curry powder will cook as well, 2 to 4 minutes.

4 Pour in the soy, vinegar, and sesame oil and continue to stir-fry the rice. Once the rice is completely hot, 3 to 5 minutes, stir in the cilantro along with the green scallion tops and serve.

VARIATION

A scrambled egg, cooked in the oil before all the ingredients get added, is usually the norm in China. Here I have kept the recipe vegan-friendly, but if you do the egg step, once the oil is hot, before you add the ginger, quickly break open a large egg and lightly beat it. Add it to the oil and you will see it instantly flare up and cook, 1 to 2 minutes. Lift the egg out of the oil and transfer it to a cutting board. Once cool, chop it up into smaller pieces or strips and add it to the fried rice before serving.

A CHINESE GEM

In 1998, I was fortunate enough to spend some time with Florence Lin, the grande dame of Chinese cooking, who taught the archetypal foods of her homeland and wrote numerous authoritative cookbooks on the subject. At a series of events for the Asian Culinary Arts Institute in Minneapolis, Florence, along with two master chefs from northern China, shared some great techniques for working with flour to shape, fill, steam, boil, pan-fry, and bake numerous varieties of buns and dumplings. At one of her sessions she sat alongside students, watching us re-create one of her recipes for baked buns with curried chicken. Being a proponent of fresh ground spices, I took it upon myself to make my own blend to replace her purchased Madras curry powder, as originally called for in the recipe. I was more than pleased with myself for creating my own version of the spice mix.

After class she approached me to applaud my dough skills but stopped short of acknowledging the freshly ground mélange in the bun's spiced chicken. "What did you think of my spice combination?" I queried because, you see, I was a bit hurt that she had not said anything specific about the flavors. With her kind yet stern voice, a reminder of her excellence as a teacher, she proceeded to educate me about the importance of using a purchased Madras curry powder for this recipe of hers.

"I grew up near Shanghai, and in my home, we only use curry from store. We never make our own. Your blend, too strong!" My assertive concoction had overshadowed the chicken pieces and that made me realize (upon further research) that purchased curry powders, a concept foreign to my Indian upbringing, enliven curries across the globe.

Flaky Curry Puffs

Piàn zhuàng gālí pào fú ·→· Makes 24 to 30 puffs

FOR THE CRUST

2 cups unbleached all-purpose flour, plus extra for dusting

¼ teaspoon coarse sea salt

8 tablespoons (1 stick) chilled butter, cut into cubes

About ¼ cup ice water

FOR THE FILLING

2 tablespoons canola or peanut oil

½ pound ground chicken

2 tablespoons finely chopped fresh ginger

1 tablespoon Madras Curry Powder (page 19)

1 teaspoon coarse sea salt

2 tablespoons soy sauce

½ cup thinly sliced white scallion bulbs

¼ cup boxed instant mashed potato flakes

1 large egg, slightly beaten

1 To make the crust, empty the flour and the salt into a food processor bowl with the metal blade in place. Add the butter to the flour. Pulse the ingredients to break up the butter into smaller and smaller pellets as the flour coats them to fashion pea-size lumps.

2 Spoon the ice water through the feeding chute and continue to pulse the machine until the dough comes together into a fairly cohesive ball. It will still be a bit loose. If it's too loose, empty the bowl's contents onto a clean board or counter. Dampen your hands and gather the dough into a tight ball, compressing it. Do not knead it as you do not want to form a lot of gluten, which will make the crust chewy. Pat it down into a patty roughly 1 inch thick. Divide the dough into two equal halves.

3 Dust one of the dough halves lightly with flour on both sides as well as the counter. Roll the dough out evenly into a rectangle roughly 6 inches x 12 inches. Gather the ends and bring them toward the center, making a trifold.

Reroll this into a square roughly 12 inches x 12 inches. Using a biscuit cutter about 3 inches in diameter, press out as many circles as possible. Stack these circles onto a flour-dusted plate, making sure each circle is dusted so as not to stick to each other. Repeat with the remaining dough half. Cover the plate with plastic wrap or a dampened paper towel (so the circles don't dry out) as you make the filling.

4 Make the filling by heating the oil in a large skillet over medium-high heat. Once the oil appears to shimmer, add the chicken and ginger and stir-fry, breaking the chicken into smaller lumps. Once they begin to cook, the chicken will resemble the texture of ground beef. This should take 5 to 6 minutes. Some of the meat and the ginger will stick to the pan.

5 Sprinkle and stir in the curry powder and salt. The heat in the cooked chicken is just right to bloom the ground spices in the blend without burning them. Turn off the heat and stir in the soy sauce, scallions, and potato flakes. Allow the filling to cool, about 10 minutes.

(recipe continues)

6 Line one (or two) sheet pan(s) with parchment paper. Get a small bowl of water ready as part of the accoutrements you will need as you start to fill the puffs. When ready to fill, cup a circle of the dough in one hand. Stick a finger in the water bowl and wet the edges of the dough about ¼ inch from the edge. Spoon a teaspoon of the cool filling into the circle's center. Fold the edges together, sealing them tight to make sure there is no opening. I usually crimp the edges with the tines of a fork. Place it on the parchment paper–lined sheet pan. Repeat with the remaining dough and filling. Make sure you place the puffs in a single layer. Brush the half-moons of filled dough with the beaten egg. Chill at least an hour in the refrigerator for the butter in the dough to cool and do its magic when baking in the oven.

7 When ready to bake, position an oven rack in the oven's center and preheat it to 400°F. Place the sheet pan with the chilled puffs directly onto the rack. Bake the puffs to a glistening gold (their color reminds me a bit of the setting sun), 20 to 25 minutes.

8 Remove them from the oven and place the sheet pan on a rack to cool, about 10 minutes.

9 I like them warm, as is, or with any dipping sauce (see Tip).

VARIATION

The day I tested this with chicken, I also made a version with mushrooms instead of the chicken. Swap ½ pound cremini mushrooms for the chicken. Pulse the fungi in a food processor to finely chop them. Proceed with the recipe.

TIP

➤ To whip up a simple dipping sauce for the puffs, in a small bowl combine ¼ cup soy sauce, ½ teaspoon toasted sesame oil, 1 trimmed, thinly sliced scallion (white bulb and green top), 1 tablespoon finely chopped fresh cilantro, and 1 to 2 teaspoons chili sauce or paste (purchased is fine) or 1 serrano chile, stem discarded, finely chopped (no need to remove the seeds).

A TIBETAN ICON

Some believe the world's tallest mountains were once covered by a massive ocean. Today we know the area as the Himalayan Mountains, where Tibet, the highest country in the world (average elevation 14,800 feet), was originally settled by people from Mongolia, China, and Burma. Their traditions are among the oldest on Earth.

Gengde was a very successful businessman in Ngaba, in Amdo province in eastern Tibet. An automobile broker who was financially thriving as he dealt in Chinese-made cars, Gengde soon felt stymied by the new Chinese authority. He wished for a better life for his family and hoped to live free. He found an opportunity to come to the United States and landed in California in 2001. Friends beckoned him to Minnesota the same year, and at last he found a home, working at a Vietnamese-inspired restaurant. He took English-language classes in a Lutheran church basement, soon learning to live in the ways of his adopted home and saving enough money to bring his family to Minnesota in 2008.

In 2010, he self-financed his restaurant, Nha Sang, a business located amid a suburban residential neighborhood. The restaurant continues to build a loyal clientele, and recently Gengde was honored to cook for the fourteenth Dalai Lama, an experience that will remain embedded in his memory forever. He realizes the restaurant is a catalyst for educating his children and also a tool to give back to the Tibetan community. Hard work and sacrifice continue to be guiding principles in his life, but he has embraced it all in pursuit of his aspirations. Even though Gengde maintains the essence of Tibetan food culture (son Sheuphen classifies it as strong, thick, plain), his menu also includes dishes from Vietnamese, Thai, Chinese, Japanese, Indonesian, and Mongolian, as well as other Himalayan cuisines to represent an amalgam of flavors that can be cohesive. Yak meat (see box, page 83), revered in Tibet, is not easy to come by in America, so beef is the standby here, pervasive and accessible.

In Gengde's experience, there is nothing more iconic in Tibet than momos, those pleated juicy dumplings filled with spiced meat or vegetables. A few years back, I had the best Tibetan dumplings in a "momo joint" in Darjeeling in northeast India, which has a large Tibetan community of immigrants and refugees. I have a chicken version here, and I find the experience of making momos quite cathartic, especially when I make the wrappers from scratch.

Steamed Chicken Dumplings with a Spiced Tomato Sauce

Momos ⋅→⋅ Makes about 24 dumplings

FOR THE DUMPLING
WRAPPERS

2 cups unbleached all-
purpose flour, plus extra
for dusting

1 teaspoon coarse sea salt

About ¾ cup boiling water

FOR THE FILLING

2 tablespoons canola oil

8 ounces ground chicken

4 ounces cremini
mushrooms, finely
chopped

2 teaspoons shredded fresh
ginger

2 teaspoons Madras Curry
Powder (page 19)

1 teaspoon coarse sea salt

½ teaspoon ground red
pepper (cayenne)

½ cup finely chopped fresh
cilantro

2 scallions, trimmed, thinly
sliced (white bulbs and
green tops)

Cooking spray

FOR THE TOMATO SAUCE

1 large tomato, cored, and
cut into ½-inch cubes

1 piece (the size of a quarter)
fresh ginger

1 fresh serrano chile, stem
removed

2 tablespoons finely
chopped fresh cilantro

2 teaspoons unrefined
granulated sugar

½ teaspoon coarse sea salt

1 Make the dumpling wrappers: Combine the flour and salt in a medium bowl.

2 Drizzle a few tablespoons of the boiling water at a time into the flour mixture, stirring the flour together with a spoon (since the water is hot, it will be difficult to use your fingers to mix the dough). Add enough water to bring the flour together to form a ball. It should feel neither sticky nor dry. Remove any dough clinging to the spoon and add it to the dough ball. Knead the dough into a smooth ball. Shape it into a log roughly 12 inches long. Cut the dough into ½-inch-wide pieces to yield about 24 pieces. Cover them up with plastic wrap until ready to shape and fill them.

3 Assemble the filling: Heat the oil in a large skillet over medium-high heat. Once the oil appears to shimmer add the chicken, mushrooms, and ginger. As it starts to cook, it will be easier to break up the ground chicken into crumbled pieces. Keep cooking, stirring occasionally, until the chicken is cooked, any excess water from the chicken has steamed off, and the mixture has taken on a reddish-brown color, 8 to 12 minutes. Sprinkle in the curry powder, salt, and red pepper. The heat in the filling will be just right to cook the ground spices without burning them, about 15 seconds.

4 Stir in the cilantro and scallions and transfer the filling to a colander set over a bowl to cool and drain any excess liquid, about 30 minutes.

5 Prepare the dumplings: Working with one piece of the dough at a time, shape it into a

(recipe continues)

marble-like round. Flatten it into a patty and roll it out into a circle 2 to 3 inches in diameter (see Note). Dust the patty with flour as needed while rolling it out. Repeat with the remaining pieces, stacking them after liberally dusting each wrapper with flour to prevent them from sticking together.

6 Place a wrapper in the palm of one hand and plop a teaspoonful of the filling in the center of the wrapper, gathering the edges over the filling to fashion a round, like an old-fashioned beggar's purse, pinching the top to seal it. (It will look almost like a Hershey's Kiss.) Lay it on a floured plate and repeat with the remaining pieces. Keep them wrapped under plastic while you quickly get the steamer together.

7 Prep a steamer basket for steaming, making sure there's enough water in the pan below to facilitate that. If you are using a bamboo steamer, line the bottom with wax paper and lightly spray the paper with cooking spray. Poke a few holes in the paper with a skewer or knife for even steaming. Bring the water in the pan to a boil over medium-high heat.

8 As the water boils in the steamer pan, place as many momos as you can in a single layer in the steamer basket, making sure they are not too close to each other (for fear of sticking together in an unwanted mass). Steam the dumplings until the dough appears opaque and dry and loses its fresh dough appearance, 10 to 12 minutes. If you have any remaining momos that did not fit the basket, repeat the steaming (making sure you add more water to the steamer pan as needed). See Note for information on freezing.

9 Make the sauce: As the momos steam, pile the tomatoes into a blender jar followed by the ginger, chile, cilantro, sugar, and salt. Puree the medley, scraping the insides of the jar for a fairly smooth puree. Transfer this to a serving bowl.

10 Serve the momos warm with the sauce on the side.

✦ *To create the perfect dough circle, I do as Florence Lin instructs in her masterpiece, Florence Lin's Complete Book of Chinese Noodles, Dumplings, and Breads: "Roll the pin with the palm of one hand while you lift and turn the wrapper with the other hand's fingers. Roll from the edges to the center so that the edges are thinner than the center." This technique may take you a few painstakingly slow tries at first, but soon, I guarantee your speed will pick up with practice. If you plan to freeze your dumplings for later use, after shaping them, lay them in a single layer on lightly floured wax paper on a tray. Freeze them on the tray for 2 to 3 hours. Once they are solidly frozen, lift them one by one and place them in a ziptop freezer bag, where they will keep for up to two months. Boil the frozen dumplings without thawing. If you don't wish to make the dumpling wrappers from scratch, nearly all Asian grocery stores and supermarkets have refrigerated or frozen packages of potsticker wrappers. Use them as a perfectly acceptable alternative.*

VARIATION

Make the filling vegetarian: Use extra-firm tofu (same amount as the chicken), drained, weighted down with a plate to release any extra moisture, and crumbled. Proceed to make the filling as instructed.

YAKETY YAK

My dear friends Brad Engdahl (retired attorney) and Pat Layton (retired psychologist), who have been to India on one of my trips, recently spent some time in Tibet. This musing from Brad on yaks in Tibet captures the essence of how the country worships this larger-than-life animal: "Yaks in Tibet provide milk, butter, butter tea, outer hair for tent fabric and rope, soft inner hair for blankets, hide for soles of boots, and dung as a basic fuel that can be seen drying in cake form on many structures. The yak also acts as a beast of burden in the treacherous Tibetan terrain. In appreciation, humans eat yak (yak steak is quite tasty). Yet yaks remain generally friendly toward humans. This is nothing short of miraculous. Given that yaks can be five feet tall, approach one ton, and have lots of energy at high altitudes (because they have triple the red blood cells of, say, a normal cow, much less a plainsman like myself), all they need is a charismatic visionary and they will rule Tibet."

THE BRITISH-JAPANESE CONNECTION

Buddhist cuisine is said to have originated in India's Mauryan empire around 200 BCE, and the Japanese adapted parts of this style by the sixth century CE. Though the Buddhists transformed Japanese cuisine with rice, sugar, tea, and other essentials, curry never caught on with the Japanese until the 1870s. Japan had maintained its independence over the years and never succumbed to the imperialistic spread that seemed to be creeping into all the surrounding countries. Japan's Meiji period (1868–1912) witnessed the opening of Japan to the rest of the globe, and it was the British merchant ships that exposed the archipelago to a whole new world of foods, including ice cream, pork cutlets, potato croquettes, and curry. This wasn't India's concept of curry but the Anglo-Indian version with its prime usage of curry powder. In Japan, curry then was never associated with Indian food, but with British fare.

Japanese curries first spread through magazines and missionary-school cookbooks and were a treat for the rising middle class—a gourmet, Western dish—but curry soon took hold in a far more common setting: military canteens. The Japanese military found curry to be one of the most "stretchable" dishes, capable of feeding thousands of sailors and soldiers, combining meats and vegetables in a kare rasu (creamy, roux-based, spiced sauce served alongside bowls of rice), fukujin-zuke (cucumber, ginger, and daikon pickled in sake, soy, and other seasonings), and rakkyo (crunchy shallots pickled in sweet vinegar). Soon school lunchrooms fed Japanese children kare raisu—especially after World War II—which appealed to their taste buds with the addition of a creamy raw egg. When curry bricks—packaged blocks of curry roux—started populating grocery store bins, households joined the craze as well, establishing curry as a definitive Japanese comfort food. Vermont Curry bricks were a version created by House Foods, the company that produced the first curry bricks, their name perhaps a nod to the inclusion of apples (which also was indicative of how the Anglo-Indians ate their curries). This was a definite kids' palate pleaser, as it wasn't hot and leaned to the sweeter side.

I would be remiss if I did not further emphasize the Japanese navy's pivotal role in shepherding the popularity of curries. Tadashi Ono and Harris Salat, in their book *Japanese Soul Cooking*, marvel at the number of "battleship curries" prepared every Friday on every ship (in containers as big as cement mixers called "shipboard cooking pots"). Each ship is known for its best recipe, which can include all sorts of unusual ingredients like red wine, instant coffee, chocolate, blueberry jam, cheese, and peaches. What is consistent among them is the accompaniments: rice; a side salad of tomatoes, lettuce, and boiled egg; and a tall glass of milk.

One of my favorite stories about Japanese curry comes from Father Patrick Okada (by way of my dear friend Richard Bresnahan). Father Patrick was originally from San Francisco; his family were tofu and pickle makers. When World War II broke out, they lost their business and were sent off to internment camps. Father Patrick got out of the camp by joining the US military to be part of the Japanese American special forces, and was trained as an interrogator in Golden Valley, Minnesota. That's where he became familiar with St. John's Abbey and University (where Bresnahan is currently the artist-in-residence), where he'd later join the monastic order. Father Patrick was a phenomenal cook, using only natural ingredients. During the war he was stationed first in India and then in Burma, where he was tasked with interrogating Japanese prisoners. On a Burmese boat that had been requisitioned by the United States, Father Patrick struck up a friendship with the Burmese cook, who made delicious curries. After watching the cook add all sorts of spices to his curries, Father Patrick turned to him and said, "You have such a beautiful brown color to your sauce. How do you get it?" The chef responded nonchalantly, "Oh, that's easy." And he picked up a bucket and threw it over the side of the ship, scooped up a bucketful of deep brown river water, and poured it into the curry. Much to Father Patrick's surprise.

The popularity of Japanese curries, in my mind, speaks to the curries' "no rules" approach. When a culture's cuisine is virtuous, moral, precise, orchestrated, devoid of spices, and beautifully presented, all while balancing flavors, colors, and cooking techniques, it is no wonder a freewheeling food like a curry has such strong appeal. Yes, Japan even had a curry museum, in the port town of Yokohama, a tribute to the naval trade that burst open the golden yellow floodgates.

Chicken Curry
with Carrots and Pickled Ginger

Kare raisu ⋅✦⋅ Serves 6

FOR THE CURRY

4 tablespoons (½ stick) butter

1½ pounds boneless skinless chicken thighs, cut into 1-inch pieces

2 large shallots, cut into ¼-inch pieces

2 large carrots, peeled, cut into ¼-inch-thick coins

2 large cloves garlic, finely chopped

2 tablespoons shredded fresh ginger

2 tablespoons S & B Oriental Curry Powder (see Tips)

1 teaspoon coarse sea salt

½ teaspoon ground red pepper (cayenne)

2 tablespoons unbleached all-purpose flour (see Tips)

3 cups chicken stock or broth

2 medium potatoes (like russet), peeled and cut into 1-inch pieces

1 cup frozen green peas (no need to thaw)

1 medium tart-sweet apple (like Granny Smith, Braeburn, or Honeycrisp), cored and cut into ¼-inch pieces

FOR SERVING

6 cups cooked sushi rice (see Tips)

Pickled ginger (see Tips)

1 Melt 2 tablespoons of the butter in a medium saucepan or Dutch oven over medium-high heat. Once it starts to foam, add the chicken pieces and allow them to brown, uncovered, stirring occasionally to ensure an even sear, 7 to 9 minutes. Transfer the chicken and any residual liquid the meat releases into a bowl.

2 If there is still some liquid left behind in the pan, allow it to evaporate before you add the remaining 2 tablespoons butter. Over the same medium-high heat, melt the butter and let it foam. Add the shallots, carrots, garlic, and ginger. Stir-fry the medley until it is light brown around the edges and smells fragrant, 6 to 8 minutes.

3 Sprinkle in the curry powder, salt, and ground red pepper, stirring to allow the spices to roast, about 10 seconds. Sprinkle in the flour as well and let it cook, stirring constantly until it is browned evenly and smells faintly nutty, about 1 minute.

4 Pour in a cup of the stock and mix it in vigorously to make sure the flour doesn't form clumps. Once the stock comes to a boil, pour in the remaining 2 cups stock, the chicken including all its pooled juices, and the potatoes. Now bring it back to a boil, uncovered. Lower the heat to medium and let the curry simmer vigorously, still uncovered, stirring occasionally, until the chicken pieces are cooked all the way through, the potatoes are fork-tender, and the sauce slightly thickens with a velvet sheen, 14 to 16 minutes.

5 Stir in the peas and the apple.

6 Serve alongside or atop the sticky rice and pass around the slices of pickled ginger for in-between nibbles.

TIPS

✦ S & B Oriental Curry Powder is, by far, the most popular brand of curry powder used in Japanese curries. It is widely available in any grocery store that stocks Asian ingredients. As you know, there are millions of curry powder blends in the world, and companies that make them hold their recipes as guarded secrets. The list of spices, in order of ingredients and proportions (from most to least), is turmeric, coriander, fenugreek, cumin, orange peel, black pepper, cayenne, cinnamon, fennel, dried ginger, star anise, thyme, bay leaves, cloves, nutmeg, sage, and cardamom. It's easy to fashion your own curry powder, and the joy is in customizing a combination that appeals to your taste buds. I use whole spices as much as I can to ensure optimum flavors, and pulverize them, untoasted, in a spice grinder (or clean coffee grinder) until they have the texture of finely ground black pepper. Also know that turmeric is most often available preground.

✦ To avoid gluten, use chickpea flour instead of all-purpose flour in the sauce.

✦ Japanese short- or medium-grain white rice, also known as sushi rice, is very starchy. You can cook it in a rice cooker or in a pot on the stove top. For a cup of sushi rice, I use 2 cups of water. Once it comes to a boil, cover it and let it steep on very low heat, until all the water is absorbed, 10 to 15 minutes. Give it a fluff before you serve.

✦ Sliced pickled ginger is pretty common in the Asian section of grocery stores. If you can't find it there, the next time you order sushi, ask for some extra pickled ginger. It's a great accompaniment to the curry.

2

AFRICA
& THE
MIDDLE
EAST

ndians influenced this expansive group of countries during ancient Babylonian times, establishing trading posts along Africa's coasts. Over the centuries, spicing techniques and combinations dotted Africa's cooking landscape and stretched into parts of the Middle East, every region painting their meats, fish, poultry, legumes, and vegetables with their signature blends. Morocco's penchant for opulent spices like grains of paradise, rose hips, and saffron; Egypt's aromatic inclusion of cloves, cardamom, and nutmeg; Ethiopia's genius technique of scenting clarified butter with toasted fenugreek seeds and cinnamon sticks to enliven every dish; Mauritius's British-influenced Madras curry powder sweetened with jaggery; and Nigeria's breathing fire into their sauces with habanero chiles—all embody the way Africa and the Middle East live into their foods: full of vigor, color, and passion.

TOASTED WHOLE SPICES
with GINGER and NUTMEG

Berbere ✦ ETHIOPIA, SOMALIA,
AND ERITREA

92

SPICED CLARIFIED BUTTER

Niter kibbeh ✦ ETHIOPIA

95

RED LENTILS with GINGER

Misir wot ✦ ETHIOPIA

97

SOUR TEFF CREPES

Injera ✦ ETHIOPIA AND ERITREA

100

LIMA BEANS with CURRY LEAVES

Cari gros pois ✦ MAURITIUS

103

SLOW-COOKED CHICKPEAS
with SAFFRON

Hommos zafaran ✦ MOROCCO

106

VEGETABLE RICE STEEPED in a ROASTED RED PEPPER– HABANERO SAUCE

Jollof rice with obe ata ✦ NIGERIA

111

LAMB POTATO STEW in BREAD BOWLS

Bunny chow ✦ SOUTH AFRICA

115

LAYERED RICE-LENTIL PILAF
with MACARONI and SPICED TOMATOES

Koshari ✦ EGYPT

118

HANDHELD EGGPLANT PIES
with a SOUR-HOT COCONUT MILK DIP

Eggplant matbucha borekas
with chamandi ✦ ISRAEL

122

FROM ETHIOPIA TO MINNEAPOLIS

Berbere is THE blend in Ethiopia, Somalia, and Eritrea, and every cook is judged on their culinary prowess based on the results of the stews and accompaniments that their spice mixture flavors. Sir Laurens Jan van der Post, a South African Afrikaner, philosopher, author, farmer, soldier, and journalist, mused about berbere in 1970: "Berbere gave me my first inkling of the essential role played by spices in the more complex forms of Ethiopian cooking. . . . It seemed to me related to that of India and of Indonesia, particularly Java. . . ." When treated to elaborate meals with raw meats, he noted that "the slices of raw meat were eaten, not undressed, but dipped in berbere, a sauce so spicy that it gives the impression of being hot enough to cook the meat; it can also transform a stew into a mixture so fierce that it practically makes the ears bleed."

Yisehak Tura, a slender Ethiopian man of 50 years, loves his life as an oncology nurse at Methodist Hospital in Minneapolis. When I asked him about his story, he said he'd grown up in an orthodox Christian home in the city of Wonji and never quite imagined he'd end up in the American Midwest. The only male child of seven children, he loved his mother's homemade fare. He recalled that she clarified spiced butter (niter kibbeh); pounded assertive spices to make her signature berbere blend; cooked stews, vegetables, and meats (usually only on the weekends) redolent with Africa's piri piri chilies; and fermented teff batter to steam piping-hot injera (see page 99). He reminisced about his mother's preparations of fiery-hot berbere sauces, also made with potent piri piri chilies, that usually draped raw meat dishes called kitfo.

As internal strife mounted within his native country, Yisehak and his wife took shelter in a refugee camp in Kenya for four years, living on rationed foreign food. Winning an immigrant lottery visa from the United States offered them new opportunities and they moved to Minnesota and started a family. Yisehak joined a nursing program and became a registered nurse, adapting and adopting American norms, as he continued to savor flavors from his homeland, now helping his wife prep and cook meals for their children. Inspired by Yisehak's story, I created this version of berbere. It may not get me a wife (or a husband), but it certainly balances some incredible flavors in a nuanced blend.

Toasted Whole Spices with Ginger and Nutmeg

Berbere ⋅►⋅ Makes ½ cup

1 tablespoon coriander seeds

2 teaspoons fenugreek seeds

1 teaspoon whole allspice

1 teaspoon black peppercorns

6 to 8 whole cloves

½ teaspoon cardamom seeds (see Tips, page 20)

4 to 6 dried red chiles (like chile de arbol), stems discarded

1 stick (about 3 inches) cinnamon, broken into 2 to 3 pieces

1 tablespoon ground annatto (achiote) seeds or sweet paprika

1 teaspoon ground ginger

½ teaspoon freshly grated nutmeg

1 Preheat a small skillet over medium-high heat. Once the pan is warm (holding your palm just above the base, you should feel heat within a few seconds), add the coriander seeds, fenugreek seeds, allspice, peppercorns, cloves, cardamom seeds, red chiles, and cinnamon pieces. Toast them, shaking the pan occasionally for an even toast, until the spices smell fragrant, the peppercorns, cloves, and cardamom appear ashy gray, the coriander and fenugreek seeds are reddish brown, and the cinnamon stick unfurls a bit, 1 to 2 minutes. Immediately transfer the spices to a plate to cool. (The longer they sit in the hot pan, the more burnt and bitter they will be.) Once they are cool to the touch, place them in a spice grinder (or a clean coffee grinder) and pulverize them until they are the texture of finely ground black pepper. Tap the lid to release any of the intoxicating blend back into the grinder's cavity.

2 Transfer this into a small bowl and stir in the annatto seeds, ginger, and nutmeg. Store this preferably in a glass jar with a tight-fitting lid in a cool spot (do not refrigerate). It will keep for up to 6 months.

ESSENTIAL JE NE SAIS QUOI

The flavors this spiced clarified butter provides in many Ethiopian dishes are that je ne sais quoi you experience when you go to an Ethiopian restaurant or someone's home to sample their fare of spiced stews and stir fries—all strategically placed on spongy injera, a bread that frankly makes me weak in the knees. Clarifying butter is not rocket science. If you can melt butter, you can clarify it—even a spiced one like this. Making this flavored variation of India's ghee from scratch in your home (which takes barely 15 to 20 minutes) is also easy on the pocketbook.

Clarified butter's nutty flavor, the result of gentle browning, is the key taste in many dishes, and often even a mere tablespoon is enough to provide succulence. It is also resistant to spoilage at room temperature, which works well in parts of Africa and India where people have less access to refrigeration. Milk solids and water promote rancidity in butter, and when they are removed, gone is the need for a refrigerator. Clarifying the butter in this way also elevates its smoke point (the temperature at which fat or oil starts to smoke), meaning you can use this butter and others for high-heat cooking and to deep-fry anything. Middle Eastern and Arabic samneh is made the same way, as is smen from North Africa.

I like to store this spiced butter in a glass jar (yes, it does look pretty) in a cool, dark spot in my pantry next to all my other oils. Refrigeration or even freezing is always an option, but for the life of me I can't imagine you won't go through that jar quickly for all your stir-frying or anointing needs.

Spiced Clarified Butter

Niter kibbeh ·•· Makes 1½ cups

| 1 teaspoon black peppercorns | 24 whole cloves | 1 pound (4 sticks) unsalted butter |
| 1 teaspoon fenugreek seeds | 4 sticks (about 3 inches each) cinnamon | |

1 Line a fine-mesh strainer with a piece of cheesecloth, set it over a clean, dry glass measuring cup (with a volume of at least 2 cups) or pint-size canning jar, and set it aside.

2 Preheat a small, heavy-bottomed saucepan over medium-high heat. Once the pan is warm (holding your palm just above the base, you should feel heat within a few seconds), add the peppercorns, fenugreek seeds, cloves, and cinnamon and toast them, shaking the pan occasionally for an even toast, until the spices smell fragrant, the peppercorns and cloves appear ashy gray, the fenugreek seeds are reddish brown, and the cinnamon sticks unfurl a bit, 1 to 2 minutes.

3 Add the butter to the pan of spices and lower the heat to medium-low. Stir the butter occasionally to ensure an even melt (otherwise, the bottom part of the block melts and starts to bubble while the top half remains firm). When it has melted and stopped foaming, skim off the foam with a spoon. Some of the milk solids will settle at the bottom and start to brown lightly. This auburn browning is essential for that nutty flavor. Allow about 25 minutes for this to happen.

4 Pour the browned butter through the cheesecloth-lined strainer, leaving the browned milk solids and the whole spices behind. Set the jar aside to cool. At this point, you can cover it for long-term storage (it will keep for months).

➤ Do *use a heavy-bottomed pan to prevent the butter from scorching. Cast iron, stainless steel, carbon steel, and ceramic-coated cast iron are all fair game. In fact, I use a cast-iron or carbon-steel wok if I happen to be making a large batch, as the fat seasons the pan.* Don't *turn up the heat beyond the low setting, as much as you may be tempted to do so; if you do, the milk solids will start to burn.* Do *make sure the glass jar is clean and dry before pouring in the niter kibbeh. Moisture will promote the growth of mold, which is the same reason why you should let it cool completely before screwing on that jar's lid.*

VARIATION: GHEE

If you wish to make unflavored ghee, the process is the same as above, except it does not involve the spices.

ETHIOPIAN COMFORT

Ethiopia, part of the Horn of Africa (which includes Eritrea, Somalia, and Djibouti), was briefly occupied by Italy under the regime of Mussolini, but remained a key part of the spice route. And it has a cuisine that relishes those aromatics and chilies with great gusto in many of its curries, stir-fries, and relishes.

The first time I sampled Ethiopian fare was in the 1990s at Blue Nile, a restaurant in my hometown of Minneapolis. The East African community there was comprised of Ethiopian immigrants and refugees who had migrated alongside families from neighboring Somalia and Eritrea to Minnesota (as well as the rest of the United States—almost half a million in all), where they were met with the foods of their upbringing. The flavor combinations at the restaurant were, to me, foreign yet familiar—and the array of lentil stews (called wats), cooked cabbage, potatoes, green beans, and a red hot paste made from a signature-blend berbere, all plopped in a graceful and colorful circular pattern on the spongy-sour injera bread, took up the small tabletop at which I was seated. Additional handkerchief-folded injera accompanied the meal, and with no silverware present, a concept that appealed to my Indian sensibilities. I tore pieces of the pancake-like bread and wrapped them around the varied morsels of delectable foods. The red lentil curry comforted my craving for my childhood's dal, but this was different: A hint of smokiness and succulence coated my palate. Years later, I mastered the techniques to re-create that dish, having learned how to roast whole spices, including black cardamom, in the butter that I clarified to cloak the quick-cooking red lentils. Serve this the way the Ethiopians do, alongside their signature bread (for homemade, see page 100) or a mound of Steeped Basmati Rice (page 193) with a drizzle of that aromatic butter.

Red Lentils with Ginger

Misir wot ·→· Makes about 3 cups

1 cup red lentils
(also known as Egyptian
lentils; see Box)

2 tablespoons Spiced
Clarified Butter (page 95)

1 medium yellow onion,
finely chopped

1 tablespoon finely chopped
fresh ginger

2 teaspoons ground Berbere
(page 92)

1 teaspoon Madras Curry
Powder (page 19)

1 teaspoon ground annatto
(achiote) seeds

1 teaspoon coarse sea salt

2 tablespoons tomato paste

2 tablespoons finely
chopped fresh cilantro

1 Measure out the lentils into a medium bowl and top it off with water. Rinse the lentils by rubbing them with your fingertips. Tilt the bowl to pour out the cloudy water. Repeat 3 to 5 times until the water after rinsing is much clearer. Drain this as well.

2 Heat the spiced clarified butter in a medium saucepan over medium-high heat. Once it appears to shimmer, add the onion and ginger. Stir-fry the medley until it is amber brown in color, about 5 minutes.

3 Stir in the ground berbere, Madras curry powder, annatto, and salt. The heat in the pan is just right to cook the ground spices without burning them. This won't take more than 15 to 20 seconds.

4 Mix in the tomato paste and add 3 cups of water along with the lentils. Bring it to a boil over medium-high heat. Then lower the heat to medium and continue simmering vigorously, uncovered and stirring occasionally, until the lentils are cooked, mushed up, and the sauce has thickened, about 20 minutes.

5 Stir in the cilantro and serve.

A CULTURE OF LENTILS

With hundreds of varieties worldwide, lentils (*Lens culinaris*) have been a part of the human diet for millennia—they were discovered in archeological remains in the Middle East dating back 8,000 years. Available in a kaleidoscope of colors, shapes, and sizes, each variety has a different cooking time. A general rule of thumb is if they are whole, they may require soaking, and if they are split, they will cook quickly even without soaking. Red (Egyptian) lentils, split in half, fall into the second category. Although the uncooked lentils have a beautiful salmon color (after their skin is hulled), they unfortunately turn yellow when cooked (don't worry, you did nothing wrong, you didn't overcook them). I have seen the red lentils at many well-stocked grocery stores and numerous supermarkets that stock legumes and spices from many cultures (some Indian stores have them labeled as masoor dal). Brownish-gray French lentils, a more common grocery store offering, will work with the flavors in this dish, if Egyptian lentils are not within reach. They will take a bit longer and an extra cup or two of water to help break them down. Split green lentils (they are actually yellow-colored with their skins washed and are called moong or mung) offer a similar texture but a very different flavor.

THE BREAD
WITH A MILLION EYES

There is nothing more fundamental than eating food with your fingers. Numerous cultures around the globe have no reason to let a fork or spoon spoil the intimacy of fingers plucking foods and delivering them to the mouth. Injera highlights this point perfectly: an edible plate with a million eyes! Spongy, soft, sour, and nutritious, this Ethiopian/Eritrean bread is pliable enough to tear with the fingers of one hand and wrap around the delectable foods that have been placed strategically on another open-faced injera. The bread is delicious and intrinsic to any Ethiopian or Eritrean meal, where it can play many different roles at once: tablecloth, plate, utensil.

Revered as the national dish of both Ethiopia and Eritrea, injera requires patience—and practice—to make. It's a project. The key to a perfect injera is fermenting the teff batter long enough to draw out its haunting sourness and give it a consistency that makes it pourable to a thin pancake. Cooking it on a flat skillet and keeping that skillet over the right temperature, one that will slowly and evenly cook the batter, is an art that becomes easier to master the more you practice. Yes, you can always buy the breads premade, which are perfectly great, but you'll miss out on the incomparable joy of making your own. You won't go wrong either way.

Sour Teff Crepes

Injera ⋅⟶⋅ Makes about 8 crepes (serves 8)

FOR THE STARTER

2 teaspoons white
  granulated sugar

1 teaspoon coarse sea salt

1 teaspoon active dry yeast

½ cup warm tap water

1 cup teff flour (see Box)

½ cup unbleached all-
  purpose flour

FOR THE CREPE BATTER

3 cups teff flour

About 2½ cups warm tap
  water

1 Combine the sugar, salt, and yeast in a medium bowl or a large (4-cup) glass measuring cup. Pour in a bit of the warm water and whisk it in completely to make sure you have no lumps forming. Stir in the remaining warm water. Add ½ cup of the teff flour and whisk it into a smooth paste. Whisk in the remaining ½ cup teff flour and the all-purpose flour until no lumps remain. Cover the starter and place it in a warm spot on the counter for about 24 hours.

2 When the starter is ready, you will see plenty of bubbling activity as it teems with yeasty presence. Now is a good time to finish the batter. Fit a stand mixer (if you have one) with the paddle attachment or a hand-held mixer with a whisk.

3 Sift the 3 cups of teff flour into the mixer's bowl or a large bowl. Scrape the starter, liquid and all, into the bowl and let the machine run on a slow speed. Carefully pour in 1 cup of the warm water and continue to beat the batter until smooth, then add another cup of warm water. At this point, the batter will still be thick. Add another ½ cup or so of the warm water and continue to beat the batter. It should

have a pourable consistency, similar to that of a slightly thick crepe batter. Once mixed, cover the bowl with a kitchen towel and place it in that same warm spot on the counter. Let sit until you see that a layer of muddy liquid has separated from the batter with bubbles rising to the top (the bubbling will be quite rampant, much like the body of a mud spring), 15 to 20 hours.

4 At this point, it is safe to start making the crepes. Give the batter a good mix to reincorporate the separated layer. It should have the consistency of a thin pancake batter; if it's too thick, add a smidgen more warm tap water. Start heating a large nonstick pan or well-seasoned cast-iron pan over medium heat. Here's the crucial part: You want your pan not too hot or cold—it must be just Goldilocks right! (If it's too hot, the batter will clump up the moment you pour it. If it's too cold, it will take forever to start cooking the batter from the underside and forming the necessary million eyes on the top side.)

5 While the pan heats, tear up a large piece of foil—about 18 inches long—and fold it in half; at this size it should be large enough to wrap up crepes that are about 8 inches in diameter. Set it next to the stove. Once the pan feels warm (holding your palm just above the base, you should feel heat within a few seconds), pour ½ to ¾ cup of the batter onto the skillet's center and quickly swirl the batter around so that it spreads evenly and forms a pancake about 8 inches in diameter. The batter will start to cook right away, acquiring an opaqueness on the top side, similar to cooking pancakes, along with lots of small air pockets (the million eyes). Cover the pan and let the injera steam for an even cooking. All this should take 2 to 3 minutes. The crepe will start to peel away from the sides of the pan. Remove it with a spatula and place it inside the prepared foil sheet, immediately wrapping it loosely to seal the moisture in, maintaining the spongy quality of the injera.

6 Sprinkle a little cold water into the pan to bring the temperature back to the right level. Repeat with the remaining batter, stacking the finished crepes on top of each other in the same foil envelope. (If you don't plan to make and consume all of the crepes at once, you can store leftover batter in the fridge, preferably in a lidded glass jar, for up to 1 week or in the freezer for 1 to 2 months.) Serve hot.

TEFF: AN HEIRLOOM SUPERFOOD

The smallest cereal grain on the planet, teff, considered a superfood, dates back to at least 4000 BCE in Ethiopia and Eritrea. Not requiring much water, teff grows in tall, feather-like grasses that turn from luminescent green to brown when ready for harvest. Commonly milled into flour, this calcium-, iron-, and protein-rich grain is readily available in health food stores or any store that caters to the Ethiopian, Somalian, or Eritrean community. Now grown and cultivated in the United States (in places like Idaho and Arizona) to supply the demand for healthy gluten-free grains, both the ivory and red grains are available, although historically the ivory variety was reserved for the Ethiopian upper class while the red was for the lower castes. This recipe uses red grains, which are more common.

FROM PARADISE, WITH LOVE

The stunning island of Mauritius, which sits in the Indian Ocean about 500 miles from Madagascar, was subjected to colonization by the Dutch, French, and British spanning more than 350 years from 1598 to 1968. The British were instrumental in bringing Indians to the island in 1843 as indentured workers (their loophole for slavery, which had been abolished by the empire by then). This is when the influence of Indian ingredients and cooking techniques took hold, swirling in flavors from China (thanks to an influx of Chinese migrants in the nineteenth century), parts of Africa Africa, the Netherlands, and France. Seafood curries and the island's tropical produce, including coconut, tamarind, and sugarcane, overflowed from many a kitchen. The Dutch and the French, before the British usurped the island, planted fruits, vegetables, and spices from faraway lands, including Brazil, India, and countries in Europe. Jean-Claude Hein, in his landmark book *Ile Maurice: Deux Siècles de Cuisine*, sheds light on its singular cuisine, which was an amalgamation of three major cuisines of the world (French, Indian, and Chinese), reflecting and a reflection of its French-Mauritian, Indian, and Chinese populations.

This particular lima bean curry, inspired by the musings from Movindri Reddy's book, *Social Movements and the Indian Diaspora*, brings in all the culinary elements of the island, including tomatoes, chilies, thyme, and the unrefined cane sugar that's called jaggery in India and piloncillo in Mexico. The British custom (in addition to its quintessential Madras curry powder) of serving curries with an assortment of toppings is reflected here as well: The lima beans come to the table adorned with raisins or apples and onion. Serve this curry the way they do in Mauritius, alongside roti dal poori (page 180), those delectable, chamois-soft flatbreads filled with spiced yellow split peas.

Lima Beans with Curry Leaves

Cari gros pois ⋅→⋅ Serves 6

1 tablespoon ghee
(for homemade,
see Variation, page 95)
or canola oil

1 teaspoon cumin seeds

1 tablespoon finely chopped
fresh ginger

2 teaspoons Madras Curry
Powder (page 19)

8 to 10 medium to large
fresh curry leaves
(see Tip, page 34)

2 large tomatoes, cored and
finely chopped

2 tablespoons coarsely
chopped jaggery or firmly
packed dark brown sugar
(see Tips)

2 tablespoons finely
chopped fresh thyme

½ teaspoon ground red
pepper (cayenne)

1 teaspoon coarse sea salt

1 package (10 ounces)
frozen lima beans, thawed
(see Tips)

¼ cup finely chopped fresh
cilantro

¼ cup golden raisins or
1 small sweet-tart apple,
cored and finely chopped

¼ cup finely chopped
red onion

1 Heat the ghee in a medium saucepan over medium-high heat. Once it starts to shimmer, sprinkle in the cumin seeds, which will start to sizzle, become reddish brown, and scent the ghee, 5 to 10 seconds. Immediately add the ginger and stir-fry until it is light brown, about 1 minute.

2 Sprinkle in the curry powder and throw in the curry leaves as the blend instantly mottles the pan with its sun-yellow presence. The heat in the ginger will be just right to cook the spices without burning them and to make the leaves splatter, 5 to 10 seconds. Yes, it's a heady aroma.

(recipe continues)

3 Stir in the tomatoes, jaggery, thyme, ground red pepper, and salt. The juicy tomatoes will start to boil and once that happens, lower the heat to medium and stew the concoction, uncovered, stirring occasionally, until the tomatoes break down a bit and appear almost saucy (although still chunky), 5 to 7 minutes.

4 Add the lima beans and 2 cups of water. Once the curry comes to a boil, lower the heat to medium and vigorously simmer it, uncovered, stirring occasionally until the lima beans are cooked and the sauce slightly thickens, 15 to 20 minutes.

5 Serve sprinkled with the cilantro, raisins, and onion.

TIPS

➤ Jaggery is sugarcane juice that has been cooked down and dried in large blocks to yield a dark brown mass, which cuts very easily with a sharp knife. It has a rich, sweet flavor with a mouthfeel similar to that of molasses. Jaggery is found in Indian, Caribbean, and Mexican grocery stores (where it is sold as piloncillo). Dark brown sugar or even molasses is a good alternative (swap them one for one).

➤ If you'd prefer to use canned lima beans, you'll need 2 cans (about 12 ounces each); drain and rinse them before use. If you plan on using dried lima beans, cook them separately in water (usually they don't need to pre-soak) and use them instead; 1 cup of dried lima beans yields 3 cups cooked.

A TOP-SHELF CUISINE

Morocco, a country in northern Africa at the mouth of the Mediterranean, has seen more than its fair share of foreign traders and colonizers over thousands of years. The Arabs, the Portuguese, and the French all left their marks on Moroccan cuisine through the introduction of techniques (like roasting meats, layering and scenting rice pilafs, and slow-cooking) and specific ingredients (like chiles and paper-thin pastry sheets). These were further inflected by the use of indigenous spices and aromatics such as saffron, mint, olives, oranges, and lemons—in total creating a singular culinary style. Morocco's iconic dishes, including tajines cooked in eponymous clay pots with chimney-like lids, in fact represent a stew of European, Mediterranean, and Moorish influences. Morocco's food culture is predominantly Islamic; meats (except pork) dominate alongside an abundance of spices, the prevalence of which can be directly traced back to the country's starring role in the spice trade.

Take, for example, one of Morocco's signature flavor blends called ras al hanout (the shopkeeper's choice mix of "top-shelf" spices and aromatics, some of which include aphrodisiacal and hallucinogenic ingredients like Spanish fly and hashish). With some blends containing anywhere from 30 to 50-plus ingredients, it is sophisticated, layered, and balanced, a close sibling to garam masalas and curry powders. It is very much an essential mélange in Moroccan bisteeya (a layered phyllo bake of minced meat scented with ras al hanout), tajines, and their infamous el majoun (sweetmeats punctuated with nuts, fruits, and an outrageous amount of spiked ras al hanout). In describing the latter in an 1846 issue of the *Revue des Deux Mondes*, the French poet Théophile Gautier (a lover of hashish) said: "The doctor stood by the side of a buffet on which lay a platter filled with small Japanese saucers. He spooned a morsel of paste or greenish jam about as large as a thumb from a crystal vase, and placed it next to the silver spoon on each saucer . . . 'This will be deducted from your share in paradise,' he said as he handed me my portion."

This layered chickpea stew is scented with my own ras al hanout (see Tips), topped with a conventional makfoul (pickled vegetables and herbs), and served over a bed of steamed, pearl-like Israeli couscous. In my not-so-humble opinion, this tajine covers all seven taste elements (hot, sour, sweet, salty, astringent, bitter, and umami), essential aromas, colors, textures, and temperatures to deliver one memorable experience.

Slow-Cooked Chickpeas with Saffron

Hommos zafaran ✦ Serves 6

FOR THE RAS AL HANOUT

1 teaspoon cumin seeds

1 teaspoon dried rose hips (or organic rose petals; see Tips)

½ teaspoon dried lavender (see Tips)

½ teaspoon grains of paradise (see Tips)

½ teaspoon cardamom seeds (see Tips, page 20)

½ teaspoon black peppercorns

½ teaspoon whole allspice

½ teaspoon mace blades

1 teaspoon ground turmeric

½ teaspoon freshly grated nutmeg

½ teaspoon ground ginger

FOR THE CHICKPEA STEW

2 tablespoons olive oil

1 large red bell pepper, stemmed, seeded, and cut into ½-inch pieces

½ cup finely chopped red onion

2 tablespoons finely chopped fresh ginger

2 tablespoons finely chopped garlic

1 tablespoon sweet paprika or ground annatto (achiote) seeds

½ teaspoon saffron threads (see Tips)

1 teaspoon coarse sea salt

1 can (14 ounces) diced tomatoes, with their juices

½ pound red potatoes, peeled and cut into 1-inch pieces (see Tips)

½ pound eggplant, trimmed and cut into 1-inch pieces

2 cans (about 15.5 ounces each) chickpeas

FOR THE SCALLION-MINT RELISH (MAKFOUL)

1 cup thinly sliced scallions (white bulbs and green tops)

½ cup finely chopped fresh mint leaves

½ cup finely chopped fresh cilantro

12 grape tomatoes, sliced in half

2 tablespoons extra virgin olive oil

1 teaspoon Maldon sea salt (see Box, opposite)

FOR SERVING

3 cups cooked Israeli couscous (see Tips)

1   To make the ras al hanout, measure the cumin seeds, rose hips, lavender, grains of paradise, cardamom seeds, peppercorns, allspice, and mace into a spice grinder (or a clean coffee grinder) and pulverize them until they are the texture of finely ground black pepper. Tap the lid to release any of the intoxicating blend back into the grinder's cavity. Transfer this to a glass jar with a tight-fitting lid and stir in the turmeric, nutmeg, and ginger. Store in a cool spot (do not refrigerate). You will have leftovers, which will keep for up to 2 months.

2   Start making the stew by heating the oil in a Dutch oven or large saucepan (or a tajine if you have one) over medium-high heat. Once the oil appears to shimmer, add the bell pepper, onion, ginger, and garlic. Stir-fry the medley until the onion is medium brown around the edges and some of the pepper pieces have patchy blisters on the skin, 6 to 8 minutes.

3 Sprinkle in 1 tablespoon of the ras al hanout spice blend along with the paprika, saffron, and salt. The residual heat of the pepper medley is just right to cook the spices without burning them. Immediately pour in the tomatoes and their juices (thus preventing the spices from burning), the potatoes, eggplant, and chickpeas and their liquid. Add 1 cup of water.

4 Bring the brothy curry to a boil. Lower the heat to medium-low and vigorously simmer the concoction, now covered, stirring occasionally, until the vegetables are fork-tender, 35 to 40 minutes.

5 Remove the lid and continue to simmer briskly, stirring occasionally to allow the sauce to thicken up a bit, the starch in the potatoes and the liquid from the chickpeas now doing their thing, 5 to 8 minutes.

6 To make the scallion-mint relish, combine all the ingredients in a medium bowl, making sure to mix well.

7 To serve, divide the couscous among individual bowls, followed by a ladleful of the chickpea stew. Top with a tablespoon of the herbaceous makfoul medley.

MY MALDON STORY

After teaching a course at the renowned King Arthur Baking School in Vermont, I picked up a box of Maldon sea salt at their store to replenish my stock back at home. As I was passing through the security line at the Boston airport to board my flight, I was pulled over by a TSA agent because of the suspicious white crystals in my bag (even though those crystals were contained inside an unopened, clearly labeled box). The supervisor was summoned and, even after I had shown a receipt, he was not convinced. Soon a drug-testing kit appeared, and the box was opened and its contents examined. Of course, the crystals did not test positive for any illicit substances, and I was cleared to board my flight—but not before the supervisor asked: "How do you use the salt?" I politely suggested he purchase one of my cookbooks for ideas and tips!

TIPS

✦ If you do not wish to make your own ras al hanout, feel free to purchase one online or from a specialty store in your area.

✦ Rose hips are the ripe fruits of the rose plant, ranging in color from red to orange to black to purple. They contain the seeds of the rose plant and add a light, perfumed, aromatic bitterness. Purchase them at any store that carries a wide range of dried spices and flowers, and get the ones that are not treated with chemicals. Dried rose petals will also do for the blend.

✦ Fresh or dried lavender drives me wild (in a good way) and is the magical ingredient that gets me to buy anything that includes it (soaps, lotions, wound disinfectants, moth deterrent for linens, cookies, chocolate, ice cream . . . you get the gist). Evocatively floral, these flowers are dried and were used by the ancient Romans (when they were in North Africa) in their baths. Specialty spice shops stock their shelves with dried lavender with great regularity. It is also a key ingredient in the French blend herbes de Provence.

✦ Grains of paradise—buttery, peppery, and with lavender undertones—are related to cardamom, ginger, and turmeric. Widely used in North Africa, originally from the Gold Coast, these are primarily available in North America in specialty spice outlets (where they are sometimes sold as melegueta or guinea pepper). I often use freshly ground grains in place of black peppercorns, with a great sea salt and butter, to dress up my tender asparagus spears or fresh green beans.

✦ Saffron, also known as zaffran or zarda, was grown and cultivated in Cyprus around 1600 BCE and later imported into the northern Indian region where Kashmir is now located. Spain is now the largest cultivator of good-quality saffron. It is the handpicked stamen of the purple blossom *Crocus sativus* and it takes about 70,000 blossoms to procure a single pound. These reddish-orange colored threads are highly aromatic, and a little goes a long way—thankfully, because it's expensive stuff. To unleash saffron's best flavor and aroma, steep it in a little hot liquid for a few minutes (I usually use cream) before use. Never buy ground saffron: It is of lesser quality and may have been adulterated with artificial colors. Also be sure to buy the spice from a reputable seller—even the threads can be modified with shredded, dyed tree bark and sold for cheap. You get what you pay for! In many cultures, turmeric is considered the poor man's saffron because it tints foods a similarly vibrant marigold color (if you wish, you can replace the saffron here with ¼ teaspoon turmeric).

✦ Keep the chopped potatoes submerged in a bowl of water. Drain and pat dry with paper towels just before using.

✦ No other ingredient has more clout than salt, dating back to prebiblical times. One of the seven essential taste elements, salt has played a key role in politics (India's Mahatma Gandhi led the salt march, a crucial movement for gaining independence from the British regime), trade (salt was used as barter for enslaved people), medicine (the Egyptians used it to embalm and mummify bodies), religion (Jesus Christ used the words "salt of the earth"), and, of course, food. It remains the pivotal player in bringing out the flavors of all the remaining six taste elements. No two sea salts (chemically speaking, sodium chloride) are the same. Each sea gifts you one with a different color and taste. The Maldon sea salt that I have called for here comes from the English coast and has thin, wide, and uneven crystals. It is a great finishing salt—that is, one added just before serving for pronounced taste and texture—that I often use on hot buttered sweet corn on the cob or steamed asparagus.

✦ A traditional Moroccan tajine is accompanied by couscous, tiny round grains of semolina, barley, or green wheat that are often steamed in a couscoussiere, a perforated pan that sits atop the tajine or stew pot. As the stew cooks beneath, the flavorful steam rises up within and cooks the grains above to a perfect fluff. Israeli couscous tends to be much larger in size, like pearl beads, and provides a rich mouthfeel. Of course, if it is unavailable in your favorite store, by all means, use the smaller-grained couscous.

✦ I do not own a tajine pot, but if you do, by all means use it to cook the stew. A Dutch oven or large saucepan, though not as romantic, works just as well.

A RIOT OF COLOR

One Friday morning, a couple of years back, I did what I always love to do—walked down the aisles of my favorite farmers' market in my hometown. Every week showcased the produce of the moment, but the tail end of summer was always my favorite when peppers of all colors and heats overflowed the baskets and bins belonging to the mostly Hmong farmers. It was a feast for the senses, and oftentimes I bought more than I could consume just so I could bask in the glory of my haul for days after. This particular morning, I came across a group of women, wrapped head to toe in fabrics that matched the riot of colors of the Scotch bonnet peppers. Within minutes they had depleted the farmer of his stock, as I stood gawking at the scene.

When it comes to food, produce, and what to do with it, I am never shy about approaching strangers with questions. After all, food is a window to a culture. These women had roots and families still in Nigeria, in western Africa, now a sovereign republic, with 160 years of British colonial rule behind it. My curiosity about their gargantuan purchase drew answers that initiated the flow of my salivary glands. One woman in particular went into ecstatic detail about the chiles in her homemade obe ata curry sauce: redolent of red bell peppers, Scotch bonnets, tomatoes, and Nigerian curry powder. As she shared her intention of making jollof rice studded with seafood, meats, and vegetables, all steeped in the curry, a mutual admiration of all things flavorful and hot grew between us, and her "rough recipe" took shape before me. My version features seasonal vegetables, but feel free to use what you have in your refrigerator or pantry. The inclusion of meats and seafood is common, very much like a paella from Spain, so if you use those, allow ample time and liquid to facilitate their cooking.

Vegetable Rice Steeped in a Roasted Red Pepper–Habanero Sauce

Jollof rice with obe ata ⋅⊷⋅ Serves 6

FOR THE OBE ATA

¼ cup canola oil or Spiced Clarified Butter (page 95)

2 large red bell peppers, cored, seeds removed, coarsely chopped

1 medium red onion, coarsely chopped

8 large cloves garlic, coarsely chopped

8 slices (each about the size of a quarter) fresh ginger, coarsely chopped

2 habanero or Scotch bonnet chiles, stems removed, coarsely chopped (no need to discard the seeds)

1 tablespoon Madras Curry Powder (page 19)

2 teaspoons ground sweet paprika or annatto (achiote) seeds

2 cans (14 ounces each) diced tomatoes, including juices, or 3 large tomatoes, cored, peeled, and coarsely chopped, including all their juices

2 teaspoons coarse sea salt

FOR THE JOLLOF RICE

1 cup white Indian or Pakistani basmati rice or jasmine rice

2 tablespoons canola oil or Spiced Clarified Butter (page 95)

1 small red onion, cut in half lengthwise and thinly sliced

1 small green bell pepper, stemmed, seeded, and cut into ¼-inch pieces

1 cup sliced fresh green beans (cut into ½-inch pieces)

1 large carrot, peeled, thinly sliced into coins

1 cup frozen green peas, thawed

1 teaspoon coarse sea salt

1 Start by making the obe ata. Heat the oil in a Dutch oven or large saucepan over medium-high heat. Once the oil appears to shimmer, add the bell peppers, onion, garlic, ginger, and chiles. Allow the vegetables to turn sunny brown and blister (the peppers in particular), stirring very occasionally, 12 to 15 minutes.

2 Sprinkle in the curry powder and paprika, stirring them in. The heat will be just right for cooking the ground spices without burning them, 10 seconds.

3 Add the tomatoes and salt, scraping the bottom of the pan to release any collected bits of vegetables, thus effectively deglazing the pan. Lower the heat to medium and cover the pan. Vigorously simmer the compote, stirring occasionally, until the chunky sauce starts to thicken a bit, about 15 minutes. Remove the lid and continue to cook away some of that liquid, stirring occasionally, until a thin layer of spiced oil glistens on its surface, 10 to 15 minutes.

4 Allow the sauce to cool a bit. Transfer half of it to a blender jar. Hold the lid down loosely with a towel as you pulse the blender and allow the steam that builds within to escape. Once you know the lid won't blow off, let the blender run to puree the sauce, scraping the insides as needed to get an even texture. It will be smooth.

(recipe continues)

Scrape its contents into a bowl. Repeat with the remaining half and add it to the first batch, giving it all a good mix to ensure an even flavor.

5 To make the rice, place it in a medium bowl. Fill the bowl halfway with water, to cover the rice. Gently rub the slender grains through your fingers, without breaking them, to wash off any dust or light foreign objects (like loose husks), which will float to the surface. The water will become cloudy. Drain this water. Repeat three or four times, until the water remains relatively clear; drain. Now fill the bowl halfway with cold water and let it sit at room temperature until the kernels soften, 20 to 30 minutes; drain.

6 Heat the oil in that same Dutch oven or large saucepan (just wiping the pan with paper towels before you heat the oil should be fine) over medium-high heat. Once the oil appears to shimmer, add the onion and bell pepper and stir-fry until the medley is light brown around the edges, 5 to 7 minutes.

7 Pile in the green beans and carrot and stir-fry the medley to partially cook it, about 5 minutes.

8 Pour in 1 cup of the prepared obe ata along with 1 cup of cold tap water. Add the drained rice as well as the peas and salt. Stir well to coat the grains with all that sauce and the vegetables.

9 Bring to a boil, still over medium-high heat. Cook until the water has evaporated from the surface and craters are starting to appear in the rice, 5 to 8 minutes. Then (and not until then) stir once to bring the partially cooked layer from the bottom of the pan to the surface. Cover with a tight-fitting lid and reduce the heat to the lowest possible setting. Steep for 8 to 10 minutes (10 minutes for a gas burner). Then turn off the heat and let the pan stand on that burner, undisturbed, for 10 minutes.

10 Remove the lid, fluff the rice with a fork, and serve.

TIPS

✦ You will have more than enough sauce left over after you use what you need for the rice. It freezes beautifully for up to 6 months, though and its versatility may very well prevent you from freezing it. Braise any meat, fish, seafood, vegetables, or grains in it. Use it as a dip for veggies or chips if you prefer. Consider it your very own simmer sauce chock-full of flavors and a pleasant underlying heat.

✦ If you use starchy, dense vegetables like potatoes, the cooking time will increase. Cut them into 1-inch cubes and allow them to cook 5 minutes longer in step 7. The amount of tomatoes in the sauce does slow down the cooking, especially of vegetables like my favorite tuber, or any other root vegetables that may suit your fancy.

NOT JUST A CUTE NAME

The Cape Malay ethnic community formed in South Africa in the mid-1600s, comprised of all the enslaved people who had been forcibly taken into South Africa from the Malay Archipelago and beyond (Indonesia, Madagascar, and India). The Cape Malays included some people from the Malay ethnic group who were forced to work in the fields, fish the waters, and fabricate carpentry, among other occupations. The women created a whole new cuisine, incorporating the spices of their heritage and the local vegetation that the Dutch colonizers had planted. In this way, the Dutch East India Company inadvertently seeded a cornucopia of dishes that came to be known as curries. Two distinct styles emerged, one that reflected the eastern part of the country and one that represented the western. Tamarind, orange leaves, star anise, and other aromatics perfumed the Cape Malay curries of the Western Cape, setting them apart from the curries influenced by the Indian laborers in the Eastern Cape and Natal. Tomatoes and assertive chiles (thanks to the Portuguese) punctuated the curries of the legacy of the Indian laborers who were persuaded by the British with promise of work and land to work the sugarcane plantations of the Natal province in the late 1700s to early 1800s.

Emblematic of the eastern, Natal curry tradition, Durban's iconic street curry—called bunny chow—can trace its roots to the businessmen and shopkeepers from the baniya (commercial merchants') community of western India, who immigrated shortly after the British took over the Cape from the Dutch East India Company. Baniya was linguistically morphed into "bunny"; "chow," unsurprisingly, referred to food. "Bunny chow" was a quintessential source of nourishment for the Black people who were prohibited during apartheid from eating at dining establishments. Mahatma Gandhi lived in South Africa and witnessed the atrocities the "coloreds" and other disenfranchised groups faced under British law, which propelled the long-fought independence movement back in India; in 1959, Martin Luther King Jr. and his wife, Coretta Scott King, would travel to India to see the place whose fight for freedom from British rule had inspired their fight for justice in the United States. During apartheid, Indian shopkeepers found a way of clandestinely feeding Black South Africans from the back door, as hearty curries stuffed into loaves of bread that required no eating utensils provided energy for the bodies that toiled the plantations under the blazing sun.

Lamb Potato Stew in Bread Bowls

Bunny chow ·→· Serves 4

FOR THE LAMB CURRY

2 tablespoons canola oil

1 teaspoon cumin seeds

3 black cardamom pods (see Note)

1 large bay leaf

1 stick (about 3 inches) cinnamon

1 medium yellow onion, finely chopped

4 large cloves garlic, finely chopped

2 tablespoons finely chopped fresh ginger

1 tablespoon Madras Curry Powder (page 19)

½ teaspoon ground red pepper (cayenne)

1 teaspoon coarse sea salt

1 pound boneless leg of lamb (sold as stew meat), cut into 1-inch pieces

1 medium potato, peeled, cut into 1-inch cubes (submerged in cold water to prevent browning; drain before use)

1 can (14 ounces) diced tomatoes, including juices

2 tablespoons finely chopped fresh cilantro

FOR THE CARROT RELISH

1 large carrot, peeled, and shredded

3 or 4 fresh green Thai or serrano chilies, stemmed and finely chopped (do not discard the seeds)

2 tablespoons finely chopped fresh cilantro

¼ teaspoon coarse sea salt

FOR SERVING

4 individual loaves of bread, like a ciabatta (or get an unsliced loaf of bread and cut it into 4 blocks)

1 Heat the oil in a medium saucepan over medium-high heat. Once the oil appears to shimmer, sprinkle in the cumin, cardamom, bay leaf, and cinnamon. Once they sizzle and scent the oil, 15 to 30 seconds, add the onion, garlic, and ginger. Stir-fry the medley until they are light brown around the edges, 5 to 7 minutes.

2 Sprinkle and stir in the curry powder, ground red pepper, and salt. The heat from the onion mélange is just right for cooking the ground spices without burning them, about 15 seconds.

3 Stir in the lamb pieces. Allow them to sear, stirring infrequently, uncovered, to seal in the juices, 3 to 5 minutes.

4 Now add the drained potatoes and continue to stir-fry the potatoes and meat to evenly cloak the pieces until they glisten with the glow of the spice blend, 1 to 2 minutes.

5 Pour in the tomatoes and their juices, scraping the bottom of the pan to release any collected browned bits of goodness, effectively deglazing the pan. Stir in 1 cup of water as well. Now bring the brothy liquid to a boil.

(recipe continues)

Cover the pan, lower the heat to medium-low, and simmer it all vigorously, stirring occasionally, until the potatoes and lamb pieces are fork-tender, 1 to 1¼ hours. The starch in the potatoes will thicken the liquid. Sprinkle in the cilantro and give it all a good stir. Remember to fish out the black cardamom pods, bay leaf, and cinnamon stick before dishing out the curry.

6 Make the carrot relish as the stew cooks by thoroughly combining the carrot, chilies, cilantro, and salt in a small bowl.

7 To serve the bunny chow, cut a slice from the top of each loaf of bread and tear out a good amount of the soft interior and reserve, leaving a cavity with about a ½-inch shell. Fill the cavities of each loaf with the lamb curry. Serve with a portion of the potent carrot medley and the torn-up whites of the bread to mop up all that succulent goodness.

VARIATION

Make it vegetarian with 2 cans (14 to 15 ounces each) red kidney beans, drained and rinsed. Follow the recipe up to Step 2. Add the kidney beans along with the potatoes and proceed with the recipe from Step 4. When simmering the beans covered, do so until the potatoes are fork-tender, about 20 minutes. Remove the lid and continue to simmer the curry, stirring occasionally, to allow the sauce to thicken, 5 to 8 minutes. Stir in the cilantro and serve the stew in the bread "bowls" as above.

✦ *Black cardamom pods, often deemed false cardamom when compared to the true green or white pods indigenous to the cardamom hills of southwestern India in the state of Kerala, are smoked during the drying process. A haunting presence in savory dishes with meats, rice, or vegetables, they provide an essential smokiness that adds depth to any dish they touch. They are available in any store that carries South Asian ingredients.*

THE SPICE MERCHANTS

Egypt, with a vibrant civilization and history going back as far as the sixth millennium BCE, experienced many a foreign influence from Greece, Persia, Rome, and, far more recently, the British. After its independence from the British empire in 1922, the country—comprising the northeastern part of Africa by the Mediterranean and Red Seas—has experienced more than its fair share of social, religious, and political struggles.

Nutmeg, cloves, and cinnamon from Asia were being used as early as 2600 BCE in the food for the laborers (commonly misconstrued to have been enslaved) who built the pyramids. Later, around 1700 BCE, cumin, marjoram, cassia, cinnamon, and anise were being imported for use in mummification. The Egyptians dominated the maritime routes between the spice countries of Asia (including the Spice Islands) and Europe around the seventh century CE. According to authors Arthur Pais and Dave DeWitt in their book *A World of Curries*, the first Asian spices were likely introduced into northern Africa by the Phoenicians, who around the eighth century BCE traveled from what is today northern Syria to establish colonies in North Africa at Carthage and modern-day Algiers. The Phoenicians carried with them spices such as nutmeg, cumin, coriander, and cloves, which together formed the basis of Middle Eastern spice blends such as baharat.

Which leads me to modern-day Egypt's national dish, koshari, a street food classic layered with pasta, rice, lentils, chickpeas, a vibrant tomato sauce, and sweet caramelized onions—all scented with that blend called baharat. Presumed to originate in concept from India's kitchiri (a risotto-like porridge of rice and lentils flavored with clarified butter and cumin seeds), via the British Raj's 30-plus year rule over Egypt and their version called kedgeree, this complete meal in a bowl took hold and soon became Egypt's go-to comfort food. The author Felipe Fernández-Armesto, in his book *Near a Thousand Tables: A History of Food*, called its colonial circulation "a phenomenon older than hamburger and fried chicken, as departing conquerors left behind an originally foreign conception of what constitutes properly soldierly food."

The long list of ingredients in the recipe may make the dish seem daunting to put together, but the beauty of it is its easy-to-execute, do-ahead quality that makes it the only star at your table. I have layered it with the spice blend every step of the way, ensuring a deep flavor that lingers with every swirl and mouthful.

Layered Rice-Lentil Pilaf with Macaroni and Spiced Tomatoes

Koshari ⋄ Serves 6

FOR THE BAHARAT SPICE BLEND

1 tablespoon coriander seeds

2 teaspoons cumin seeds

2 teaspoons black peppercorns

½ teaspoon whole cloves

½ teaspoon cardamom seeds (see Tips, page 20)

2 sticks (about 3 inches each) cinnamon

2 tablespoons ground annatto (achiote) or sweet paprika

1 teaspoon freshly grated nutmeg

FOR THE CARAMELIZED ONION AND SAUCE

4 tablespoons extra virgin olive oil

2 cups cubed red onion (in ½-inch cubes)

5 medium cloves garlic, finely chopped

1 can (15 ounces) tomato sauce

½ teaspoon coarse sea salt

½ teaspoon ground red pepper (cayenne)

FOR THE LENTILS AND RICE

½ cup dried French lentils

½ cup white basmati rice (preferably Indian or Pakistani) or long-grain rice

1 teaspoon coarse sea salt

½ cup dried macaroni

1 can (about 15 ounces) chickpeas, drained and rinsed

1 Start by making the baharat spice blend. Preheat a small skillet over medium-high heat. Once the pan is warm (holding your palm just above the base, you should feel heat within a few seconds), add the coriander, cumin, peppercorns, cloves, cardamom, and cinnamon and toast them, shaking the pan occasionally for an even toast, until the spices smell fragrant, the peppercorns, cloves, and cardamom appear ashy gray, the coriander and cumin seeds are reddish brown, and the cinnamon sticks uncurl a bit, 1 to 2 minutes. Immediately transfer the spices to a plate to cool. (The longer they sit in the hot pan, the more burnt and bitter they will be.) Once they are cool to the touch, place them in a spice grinder (or a clean coffee grinder) and pulverize them until they are the texture of finely ground black pepper. Tap the lid to release any of the intoxicating blend back into the grinder's cavity.

2 Transfer the ground spice blend to a glass jar with a tight-fitting lid and stir in the annatto and nutmeg. Store in a cool spot (do not refrigerate). You will have leftovers, which will keep for up to 2 months.

3 To caramelize the onion (and this is really about slow cooking and a color intensely chocolate brown), bring 2 tablespoons of the oil to a shimmering stage over medium heat in a large skillet. Dump the onion into the skillet, turn the heat to medium-low, and cook, uncovered and stirring occasionally, until the pieces are deep caramel brown, almost crispy (especially around the edges), and you will know just by looking at them that the sugar is beyond containment within these pieces, about 30 minutes.

4 Make the sauce by heating the remaining 2 tablespoons of oil in a small saucepan over medium heat. Once the oil appears to shimmer, stir-fry the garlic until light brown and fragrant, 1 to 2 minutes.

5 Carefully pour in the tomato sauce (making sure you get every last bit of it from the can) and stir in 2 teaspoons of the baharat spice blend, plus the salt and ground red pepper. Now reduce the heat to low and simmer the sauce, covered, stirring occasionally, until the sauce acquires a deep, rich reddish-brown color with a thin layer of spiced oil on its surface, 25 to 30 minutes.

6 Meanwhile, wash the lentils under water (a fine-mesh colander works great), drain, and transfer them to a medium saucepan. Add 4 cups of water and bring to a boil. Give them a stir or two and lower the heat to medium-low. Cover the pan and brisk-simmer the lentils, stirring occasionally, until they are tender but not mushy, about 30 minutes. Scoop the lentils out into a medium bowl and set it aside; reserve the lentil water.

7 To prepare the rice, measure it into a small saucepan. Fill the pan with water to cover the rice. Gently rub the slender grains between the fingers of one hand to wash off any dust or light foreign objects (like loose husks), which will float to the surface. The water will become cloudy; drain it (I just tip the pan over the sink to pour it off, making sure the rice stays in the pan). Repeat three or four times, until the water remains relatively clear; drain. Now pour in ¾ cup cold tap water and let it sit at room temperature until the grains soften, 10 to 15 minutes. Do not drain.

(recipe continues)

8 Bring the water and rice to a boil over medium-high heat. Stir the rice once or twice (just because) and allow the water to boil, uncovered and undisturbed, until it has evaporated from the surface and craters are starting to appear in the rice, 5 to 8 minutes. Now (and not until now) stir once or twice to bring the partially cooked layer from the bottom of the pan to the surface. Cover the pan with a tight-fitting lid and reduce the heat to the lowest possible setting. Steep for 5 to 8 minutes (8 for an electric burner, 5 for a gas burner). Then turn off the heat and let the pan stand (or sit, for that matter), undisturbed, for an additional 5 minutes.

9 Uncover the pan, fluff the rice with a fork (this lets the steam escape, so it does not overcook the rice), and add this to the bowl with the lentils. Sprinkle in 1 teaspoon of the baharat spice blend and ½ teaspoon of the coarse sea salt and give it all a good stir.

10 Add water to the reserved lentil water to equal about 4 cups (you want enough water to cook the ½ cup macaroni). Bring to a boil and cook the macaroni per the package instructions until it is al dente (toothsome and not mushy); do not drain. Now add the chickpeas to the macaroni and water to warm them for a moment, then drain into a colander, giving the colander a good shake, and transfer the macaroni and chickpeas to a medium bowl. Sprinkle in a teaspoon of the baharat spice blend along with the remaining ½ teaspoon coarse sea salt. Give it a good mix.

11 For each serving, lay a portioned bed of the rice–lentil pilaf and follow it up with some of the chickpeas and macaroni. Ladle on a scoop of the sauce and top it off with some of the sugary-sweet onion. Give it all a good mix with your fork and dig in. Any leftovers will keep in an airtight container in the refrigerator for up to 2 days.

ISRAEL'S COCHIN DELICACIES

Associating Israel with India might be surprising, but when you understand the historical presence of the Jewish community in India (now very much dwindling), it all makes sense. Three groups of Jews arrived in India at various times: The earliest of them—called the Bene Israelis (early first and second century CE)—arrived at the Konkan coast just south of Bombay (now Mumbai). They were followed by the Cochini Jews (around the second century CE), who settled in Cochin in the southwestern state of Kerala; many of their ancestors moved back to Israel in the 1950s and early '60s. In the eighteenth century, both groups were joined by Baghdadi/Sephardic Jews from the Jewish diasporas around the Indian Ocean and the Mediterranean and from Iraq.

I first became intrigued by the India–Israel connection thanks to an article by Dana Kessler in the *Tablet* that profiled a group of women who live in Nevatim, Israel, whose ancestors were Black Cochini Jews. These eight women operate a food establishment called Matamey Cochin ("Cochin Delicacies"), serving meals that keep the flavors of Cochin (now Kochi) alive, their dishes punctuated with mustard seeds, curry leaves, cardamom, cinnamon, cumin, coriander, bell pepper, and coconut milk. These are not conventional meals from Kerala, but foods of Israel like pastels, borekas, kubbeh, and matbucha accented with some of the Indian spices. Observing kosher means avoiding a mix of dairy and meats, so the coconut milk is paramount, a perfect stand-in for cream and milk.

My creation is a celebration of those foods and flavors, all neatly cocooned in pastry, served with Matamey Cochin's signature chamandi sauce, sour and hot, full of addictive flavors. And no, you can't just have one boreka.

Handheld Eggplant Pies
with a Sour-Hot Coconut Milk Dip

Eggplant matbucha borekas with chamandi ⇢ Makes about 30 borekas

FOR THE CRUST

2 cups unbleached all-purpose flour, plus extra for dusting

¼ teaspoon coarse sea salt

8 tablespoons (1 stick) chilled butter, cut into cubes

About ¼ cup ice water

FOR THE FILLING

1 medium eggplant (about 1 pound)

1 large red bell pepper

1 to 2 serrano or jalapeño chiles

1 medium tomato

1 teaspoon cumin seeds

Seeds from 4 green or white cardamom pods (see Tips, page 20)

1 teaspoon coarse sea salt

2 tablespoons canola or coconut oil

1 large egg, slightly beaten

FOR THE DIPPING SAUCE

1 tablespoon canola or coconut oil

½ teaspoon black or yellow mustard seeds (see Tips)

1 serrano chile, stem removed, finely chopped (do not discard the seeds)

4 to 6 medium to large fresh curry leaves (see Tips, page 34)

2 tablespoons ground blanched almonds (see Tips)

1 cup unsweetened coconut milk

½ teaspoon tamarind paste or concentrate, or juice from 1 small lime (see Tips)

½ teaspoon coarse sea salt

1 To make the crust, empty the flour and the salt into a food processor bowl with the metal blade in place. Add the butter to the flour. Pulse the ingredients to break up the butter into increasingly smaller pellets as the flour coats them to fashion pea-size lumps.

2 Spoon the ice water through the feeding chute and continue to pulse the machine until the dough all comes together into a fairly cohesive ball. It will still be a bit loose. If it's a tad bit dry to pick up, wet your hands first—that will provide enough moisture to gather it all together. Empty the bowl's contents onto a clean board or counter. Gather the dough into a tight ball, compressing it. Do not knead it, as

you do not want to form a lot of gluten (it will make the crust chewy). Pat it down into a patty roughly 1 inch thick. Divide the dough into two equal halves.

3 Dust the counter with flour and then dust one of the dough halves lightly with flour on both sides. Roll it out evenly into a rectangle roughly 6 inches x 12 inches. Gather the ends and bring them toward the center to fashion a trifold. Reroll this into a square roughly 12 inches in size. Using a biscuit cutter, about 3 inches in diameter, press out as many circles as possible. Stack these circles onto a flour-dusted plate, making sure each circle is dusted so as not to stick to one another. Repeat with the remaining dough half. Cover the plate with plastic wrap or a dampened paper towel (so the circles don't dry out) while you make the filling.

4 Make the filling by first preheating a gas or charcoal grill, for indirect grilling over high heat. Alternatively, preheat the broiler to high.

5 Prick the eggplant in multiple spots with a fork or knife (this prevents it from bursting when you grill or broil it). Don't bother to remove its stem, since it will be discarded when you skin the eggplant. *If you are grilling*, place the eggplant, bell pepper, chiles, and tomato on the grill grate away from the flame. Cover the grill and cook the vegetables, turning them periodically to ensure even grilling, until their skins are evenly charred,

about 25 minutes. The tomato and the chiles may be done sooner, so remove them and set them in a large bowl. *If you use the broiler*, position the broiler rack so the eggplant, bell pepper, chiles, and tomato will be about 6 inches from the heat. Place the vegetables on the rack and broil them, turning them periodically, until their skins are evenly charred, about 25 minutes. The tomato and the chiles may be done sooner, so remove them and set them in a large bowl.

6 Add the eggplant and bell pepper to the chiles and tomato. Cover the bowl with plastic wrap, and let the vegetables sweat in their own heat until the skins appear shriveled, about 15 minutes. Once the eggplant and the remaining vegetables are cool to the touch,

(recipe continues)

TIPS

✦ Part of the Brassica family (cabbage, broccoli, cauliflower), mustard plants are a cash crop in many cultures and their beautiful yellow flowers bring sunshine to their fields. The leaves, seeds, and oil are all prized in cooking. Three varieties of mustard plants are harvested for their seeds: *Brassica nigra*, *B. juncea*, and *B. alba*. The seeds contain glycosides that impart the sharp bitterness associated with mustard. When you pop the seeds in hot oil, they will turn nutty and popcorn-like in aroma, but if you let them stay in that hot oil for a while, their bitterness comes through (that's why I call them the Dr. Jekyll and Mr. Hyde of the spice world).

✦ I use my handy spice grinder (or a clean coffee grinder) to grind this small amount of almonds. Don't let it grind away for a long time, since the almonds can release their oils and gum up the powder.

✦ Native to Africa but found in prehistoric fossilized remains in India, the tamarind tree grows wild in many tropical climates across the world. The olive green pods, which look like fat pods of beans, house the tart fruit within which you can find the seeds of the tree. As kids, we collected those seeds and played board games with them. The fruit, once it's been soaked and had its juices extracted, sours many a stir-fry, stew, curry, and relish. Specialty markets and even the produce aisle of mainstream grocery stores stock these pods and the more convenient tamarind paste or concentrate. An addictive candy is the mashed tamarind fruit studded with sugar, appealing to your sweet-sour taste buds. The sourness is complex, but if tamarind is unavailable where you are, lime or lemon juice imparts that taste (but not the complexity).

peel them and discard the stems along with the skins. You don't need to discard the seeds from the chiles or the tomatoes, but please do so from the red bell pepper. You will notice that there are eggplant juices in the bowl—reserve them. Mash the eggplant and the vegetables well with a potato masher or a clean hand. Set aside.

7 Preheat a large skillet over medium-high heat. Sprinkle in the cumin and cardamom seeds, which will start to smell fragrant and change color, 10 to 15 seconds. Transfer this to a spice grinder (or a clean coffee grinder). Once the spices are cool, grind them to the texture of finely ground black pepper. Tap the lid to release any of the intoxicating blend back into the grinder's cavity. Add the blend along with the salt to the mashed vegetables. Give it all a good mix.

8 Add the oil to that same skillet, again over medium-high heat. It should start to shimmer right away. Add the spiced vegetables and roast them, uncovered, stirring occasionally until all of the liquid dries up, 10 to 15 minutes. Transfer this mixture to a colander set over a bowl or the sink to get rid of any remaining liquid.

9 Line a sheet pan (or two) with parchment paper and fill a small bowl with water. Cup a circle of the dough in one hand. Stick a finger in the water bowl and wet the edges of the dough about ¼ inch from the edge. Spoon a teaspoon of the cool filling in the circle's center. Fold the edges together, sealing them tight to make sure there is no opening. I usually crimp the edges with the tines of a fork. Place it on the parchment paper–lined sheet pan. Repeat with the remaining dough and filling. Make sure you place the borekas in a single layer. Brush the half-moons of the filled pies with the beaten egg. Chill at least an hour in the refrigerator to allow the butter in the dough to cool and do its magic when baking in the oven.

10 When ready to bake, position an oven rack in the oven's center and preheat it to 400°F. Place the sheet pan with the chilled pies directly onto the rack. Bake them to a glistening gold (the color reminding me a bit of the setting sun), 20 to 25 minutes. Remove them from the oven and place the sheet pan on a rack to cool, about 10 minutes.

11 While the borekas bake, make the dipping sauce. Heat the oil in a small saucepan over medium-high heat. Once the oil appears to shimmer, sprinkle in the mustard seeds, which will start to pop almost instantly. Once they start popping, place a lid on the pan to contain them. As soon as they finish popping, remove the lid to experience the popcorn nuttiness, about 30 seconds. Immediately stir in the chile, curry leaves, and almonds. As soon as the almonds brown, about 30 seconds, carefully pour in the coconut milk and stir in the tamarind and salt. Bring it to a boil and allow the sauce to thicken a bit and the flavors to mingle, uncovered, stirring occasionally, 3 to 5 minutes.

12 Serve the borekas warm alongside the dipping sauce.

coriander

3

EUROPE &
OCEANIA

RICE

I t's not hard to see the influence of curry in the cuisines of Europe. From the signature dishes of Venice, Italy, scented with aromatic spices like cinnamon and cardamom, to the ubiquitous chicken tikka masala (a dish that feels quintessentially Indian to so many despite its debated origins in the Glasgow kitchen of a Bangladeshi chef), curry makes its redolent presence known.

After all, the European taste for spices dates from the time of the ancient Greeks and Romans who acquired cinnamon, cardamom, ginger, and the like, first from Arab traders and then from Romans who began trading with India. Following the decline of Rome, Italian city-states began dealing in spices, with Venice becoming dominant. To break Venice's hold on this lucrative business and to avoid the dangers of the overland routes, fifteenth- and sixteenth-century European rulers began to search for ways to procure spices directly—going to the sources by way of the sea, beginning what became known as the Age of Discovery. Portuguese, then Spanish and Dutch explorers reached Asia where they sought to control spice markets by whatever means they could, often by force and other exploitative methods. One result was that spices became more affordable to Europeans who began incorporating them into everyday dishes. Returning explorers also brought back a taste for the foods they had found in their travels. Both factors no doubt laid the groundwork for the presence of curries, as well as the invention of new curries, throughout the budding modern world.

Though curry's roots took hold in Oceania later than they did in Europe, thanks to multiple immigration channels from Europe and Asia, its foothold in the cuisine is clearly seen in dishes that have become widely embraced and beloved, like the goat curry popular in the Fijian archipelago today. Curry, I so emphatically believe, reinforces lasting connections among diverse cultures wherever it goes.

PORK MEATBALLS
in a CREAMY CURRY SAUCE

Boller i karri ✦ DENMARK

130

YOGURT-MARINATED
CHICKEN THIGHS
with CREAMY TOMATO SAUCE

Chicken tikka masala ✦ UNITED KINGDOM

133

CURRIED DEVILED EGGS

UNITED KINGDOM, UNITED STATES

136

CREAMY CHICKEN VEGETABLE
SOUP with APPLES

Mulligatawny ✦ UNITED KINGDOM

139

BRITISH CURRY HOUSE
VINDALOO

Pork vindaloo ✦ UNITED KINGDOM

142

CORONATION CURRIED
CHICKEN SALAD with
APRICOTS

UNITED KINGDOM, UNITED STATES

143

PASTA with PINE NUT– and
RAISIN-MARINATED
SARDINES

Bigoli con saor sarda ✦ ITALY

147

SPINACH and OLIVE QUICHE
with RAS AL HANOUT

FRANCE

150

SAUSAGES SMOTHERED
in a SPICED KETCHUP

Currywurst ✦ GERMANY

153

CRISPY VEGETABLE
CURRY TRIANGLES

Chamuça ✦ PORTUGAL

155

CREAMY CURRIED
SCALLOP PIES

AUSTRALIA

159

GOAT CURRY
with AMARANTH GREENS

FIJI

162

DENMARK'S COMFORTS

I would never have imagined that the people of Denmark loved curries and spices, but then why would it be a surprise? As part of Scandinavia in northern Europe and, prior to 1814, an ally of Norway, Denmark was a colonial presence in southern India for 200 years. But the Danes were never really as important in the spice trade as the English and Dutch were. Their food culture was dictated by the short growing season and ways to extend it that were and are reflected in their techniques of drying and smoking meats and fermenting fish such as herring. Of course, the strong flavors and robust tastes that result from those techniques lend themselves well to curry powders and other spices like allspice, peppercorns, cumin, fennel, cardamom, cloves, cinnamon, saffron, and ginger—ingredients Danes imported from the players along the spice route.

Their curries were and are simple, still very much relying on the catch-all curry powder, nothing too complicated or layered. One spice that to this day signifies Scandinavian cooking—especially baking—is cardamom, a procurement from the Venetian spice route and no surprise because of Denmark's experiences in southern and southeastern India. Living in Minnesota, a state where Scandinavian culture and flavors dominate, I have been fortunate to sample those flavors, particularly the heady cardamom cookies baked during the winter holidays.

Pickled herring soaked in mayonnaise and curry powder is a favorite in Denmark, as are these tender pork meatballs bathed in a curry sauce, Anglo-English style, roux and all, replete with apples and fresh dill. Serve this well-loved comfort food the way the Danes do: over steeped white rice. Especially when you live in cold climates, this combination warms your body and spirit.

Pork Meatballs in a Creamy Curry Sauce

Boller i karri • Serves 6

FOR THE MEATBALLS

1 pound ground pork

1 small yellow onion, finely chopped

2 large cloves garlic, finely chopped

1 cup plain or seasoned breadcrumbs

1 teaspoon coarse sea salt

½ teaspoon coarsely cracked black peppercorns

½ teaspoon ground allspice

1 large egg, slightly beaten

4 cups low-sodium chicken stock or broth

FOR THE CREAM SAUCE

2 tablespoons butter

1 large leek, washed well, beard discarded, and finely chopped (white bulb and light green top)

2 tablespoons unbleached all-purpose flour

2 teaspoons Madras Curry Powder (page 19)

½ teaspoon coarse sea salt

½ cup heavy (whipping) cream

2 tablespoons finely chopped fresh dill

1 small sweet-tart apple (like Granny Smith, Honeycrisp, or Braeburn), cored, finely chopped

3 cups cooked long-grain white rice (see page 193)

1 Place the pork in a medium to large bowl and add the onion, garlic, breadcrumbs, salt, pepper, allspice, and egg. Thoroughly combine the pork and the flavorings to make sure the meat is well seasoned. Refrigerate the pork to chill it so it will be a bit easier to scoop out and shape into meatballs, about 30 minutes. If you do this overnight, let it rest at room temperature for a few minutes to eliminate the excess chill.

2 Grab a tablespoon of the pork and shape it into a ball, compressing the meat a bit between the palms to fashion a cohesive and compact round. Place it on a plate. I prefer the meatballs a bit smaller as they tend to be more tender and will absorb the sauce's flavors so much better. Finish shaping all of them.

3 Pour the chicken stock into a Dutch oven or large saucepan and bring it to a boil over medium-high heat. Lower the heat to medium and add the meatballs to the pan. Simmer them vigorously, uncovered, stirring occasionally and carefully, and cook all the way through, 8 to 10 minutes. Remove them with a slotted spoon onto a clean plate. Reserve 2 cups of the pork-flavored stock remaining in the pan. If there is extra left over, save it for another project; it will keep frozen for at least a month.

4 To make the sauce, wipe the pan dry or dry it off over medium heat. Once dry, melt the butter over medium heat and then add the leek. Stir-fry the leek to barely remove its pungency, 2 to 4 minutes.

5 Sprinkle in the flour and continue to cook the ingredients to allow the flour to roast and turn ever so slightly brown, 1 to 2 minutes. Add the curry powder and stir it in; the heat in the roux is just right to cook the spices without burning them, about 1 minute.

6 Pour in the reserved stock, a little at a time, and whisk it in to make sure you have a lump-free sauce. Add the salt and the pork meatballs (including any residual juice). Let

the sauce and meatballs simmer vigorously, uncovered, stirring gently and occasionally to allow the sauce to thicken, 6 to 8 minutes.

7 Pour in the cream and continue to simmer the curry to warm the cream and to allow it to thicken ever so slightly, 3 to 4 minutes.

8 Stir in the dill. Serve the creamy meatballs in bowls with the apple and rice alongside for folks to help themselves.

A BRITISH INVENTION

In 2001, when he was Britain's foreign secretary, the late Robin Cook declared chicken tikka masala a "true British national dish," much to the shock of some food critics. They deemed it "inauthentic" since it was created by a Bangladeshi cook in Glasgow to appease a customer who complained that the chicken tikka he had been served was too dry. In fact, the authentic version of the dish had no sauce. Babur, India's premier Mughal emperor, was responsible for having his cooks in India create chicken tikka, bite-size boneless morsels marinated in yogurt and spices and grilled in a tandoor, sans sauce. So the Bangladeshi cook added Campbell's tomato soup to the chicken, fortified it with spices and cream, and presented a curry that would surely appease the irate client. And thus the dish took on a personality of its own in Britain, then spread to the rest of the United Kingdom and the world.

I find this version of mine particularly pleasing, as the heat from the sweet paprika is mellow and does not take away from the sauce's delicate, nutty, creamy tastes.

Yogurt-Marinated Chicken Thighs with Creamy Tomato Sauce

Chicken tikka masala ·•· Serves 4

FOR THE CHICKEN

½ cup Greek-style plain yogurt

6 slices (each the size of a quarter) fresh ginger

4 large cloves garlic

2 tablespoons finely chopped fresh cilantro

2 teaspoons coriander seeds, ground

1 teaspoon cumin seeds, ground

2 teaspoons ground sweet paprika

1½ teaspoons coarse sea salt

½ teaspoon ground turmeric

1½ pounds boneless skinless chicken thighs, cut lengthwise into 1-inch-wide strips

FOR THE SAUCE

2 tablespoons ghee (homemade, page 95, or purchased) or unsalted butter

1 small red onion, coarsely chopped

1 small red bell pepper, halved lengthwise, stem and seeds removed, and cut into ½-inch pieces

¼ cup raw cashew nuts

¼ cup golden raisins

1 tablespoon Madras Curry Powder (page 19)

1 cup canned diced tomatoes, including juices

1 tablespoon tomato puree

¼ cup heavy (whipping) cream or half-and-half

½ teaspoon coarse sea salt

¼ teaspoon ground red pepper (cayenne)

Cooking spray

2 tablespoons finely chopped fresh cilantro

1 Marinate the chicken: While the skewers soak (see Note), spoon the yogurt into a blender jar along with the ginger, garlic, cilantro, ground coriander, ground cumin, paprika, salt, and turmeric. Puree the marinade, scraping the inside of the jar as needed, to a slightly gritty but smooth consistency. Scrape this thick marinade, mottled with spices the color of the setting sun, into a medium bowl. Add the chicken strips to this, giving it all a good mix to completely coat the chicken. Refrigerate, covered, at least 30 minutes or up to 6 hours.

2 Make the sauce: Heat the ghee in a small saucepan over medium-high heat. Add the onion, bell pepper, cashews, and raisins to the pan. Cook, stirring frequently, to allow the vegetables to gently sweat and then start to lightly brown as they soften and acquire light honey-brown patches. The nuts and raisins will turn reddish-brown, and a thin film of brown will coat the pan's bottom, 10 to 12 minutes. Cooking the vegetables in a smaller pan allows them to sweat a little to create moisture that prevents the pan's contents from blackening.

(recipe continues)

3 Sprinkle and stir in the curry powder. The heat will be just right in the pan to cook the spices without burning them. Stir in the diced tomatoes along with the tomato puree, and scrape the pan to release any browned bits of vegetables and raisins to effectively deglaze it. Pour this chunky sauce into a clean blender jar along with the cream, salt, and ground red pepper. Puree, scraping the inside of the jar as needed, to make a thick, nutty-gritty sauce, reddish-brown in color with a slight kick to it, thanks to the ground red pepper.

4 Pour the sauce into a medium saucepan and simmer it on low heat, covered, stirring occasionally, while you grill the chicken.

5 Skewer and grill the chicken: Preheat a gas or charcoal grill for direct heat or the broiler.

6 While the grill heats, thread the chicken strips (the marinade is quite thick so you should not have any residual marinade), accordion style, onto the skewers. Lightly spray the grill grate with cooking spray. Grill the chicken, covered, turning the skewers occasionally, until the pieces are reddish brown and the insides, when cut, are no longer pink and the juices run clear, 6 to 8 minutes. *If broiling*, lightly spray the broiler rack with cooking spray. Place the skewered chicken on the rack. Broil with the tops 2 to 3 inches from the heat, turning the skewers occasionally, until the pieces are reddish brown and the insides, when cut, are no longer pink and the juices run clear, 6 to 8 minutes.

7 Strip the chicken off the skewers into the sauce. Stir once or twice to make sure the sauce drenches the tender juicy meat.

8 Serve sprinkled with the cilantro.

✦ *You will need bamboo skewers soaked in water for an hour to prevent burning (you can do this while you marinate the chicken), or metal skewers.*

DEVIL'S FOOD

Laura Schumm, in her article "Ancient History of Deviled Eggs," credits the Romans, as early as the fourth and fifth century CE, with boiling eggs and flavoring the yolks with spices and herbs like pepper, lovage, and even pine nuts. Banquets around 61 CE showcased stuffed eggs as starters. An often-used Latin phrase "ab ovo usque ad mala" ("from egg to apples") emphasized the importance of beginning full-course meals with eggs prepared in this fashion. Cooks in Andalusia (now Spain) in the thirteenth century mixed the yolks from boiled eggs with cilantro, pepper, coriander seeds, and onion (all essential ingredients to a good curry), but credit goes to Great Britain for starting to call eggs that were spiced and hot "deviled" in the late 1700s. When these spice-stuffed eggs became standard fare at church suppers and gatherings, where the word "deviled" was forbidden, it was replaced with "salad," "stuffed," or "dressed." The credit for including mayonnaise as a creamy binder for the boiled egg yolks goes to the United States—specifically Fannie Farmer's iconic 1896 *Boston Cooking-School Cook Book*—and ever since, cooks have been whipping their yolks with mayo and all kinds of flavors, including the emergence of the "exotic" British-invented curry powder, bringing home the tastes of the subcontinent. A conversation starter indeed at gatherings and parties!

My take on curried deviled eggs goes beyond just dusting or incorporating raw curry powders into the scooped egg yolks. I know that uncooked curry powders leave behind a chalkiness that results in an unpleased palate. The simple technique of stir-frying scallions in butter provides just the right amount of heat to cook the blend without burning it. Yes, my recipe pays homage to all the previous renditions of this popular starter, but it also elevates it with the grassy freshness of dill, a silent nod to the early Romans who used its sibling lovage.

Curried Deviled Eggs

Makes 8 halves

4 large eggs (see Tip)

½ teaspoon baking soda

1 tablespoon butter

1 large scallion, trimmed, white bulb finely chopped, green top thinly sliced (keep separate)

2 teaspoons Madras Curry Powder (page 19)

2 tablespoons crème fraîche or sour cream

1 tablespoon mayonnaise

1 tablespoon Dijon mustard

1 tablespoon white wine vinegar

1 tablespoon finely chopped fresh dill

½ teaspoon coarse sea salt

½ teaspoon coarsely cracked black peppercorns

1 Place the eggs carefully in a small saucepan side by side so they don't crack with your rough handling. Add cold tap water to cover by a depth of at least an inch. Add the baking soda to the water. Bring it to a boil over medium-high heat. Turn off the heat. Cover the pan and allow the eggs to gently cook in the hot water, undisturbed, 15 minutes.

2 Fill a medium bowl halfway with cold tap water and add a cup of ice to it. Remove the cooked eggs gently from the pan with a slotted spoon and lower them into the ice bath. Let the eggs chill, until cool to the touch, about 10 minutes, then peel and discard the shells. Slice the eggs in half and scoop the yolks into a small bowl, leaving behind a hollowed interior and a velvet-smooth egg white.

3 Meanwhile, heat the butter in a small skillet over medium heat. Once the butter melts and foams around the edges, add the white scallion bulb to it. Stir-fry to scent the butter, until the scallions are a bit limp (not brown), 1 to 2 minutes. Turn off the heat and sprinkle in the curry powder. The heat will be just right to cook the spices without burning them. Place the egg whites face down into the spiced butter as you get the filling ready.

4 To the scooped egg yolks, add the crème fraîche, mayonnaise, mustard, vinegar, dill, salt, pepper, and the green scallion tops. Remove the egg whites onto a plate, placing the spiced side up. Scrape the spiced butter from the skillet into the bowl along with the filling ingredients. Beat the filling to a smooth and whipped consistency (still slightly chunky but creamy and airy).

5 Fill and mound each egg white generously with the filling, making sure to cover almost up to the edges. Serve at room temperature (they will keep for 1 hour) or chill in an airtight container in the refrigerator (they will keep for a few days).

TIP

✦ The eggs for this dish should be not too fresh—use ones that have been sitting in your fridge for at least a few days. They will be easier to peel once hard boiled.

AN ENGLISH ICON

The night's meal in my mother Amma's kitchen had four guarantees: The family ate together; shaadum (rice) was a must; some type of a sambhar (stew) or a rasam (soup) made its appearance; and the meal always culminated with yogurt or buttermilk. My favorite was invariably the rasam: watery thin, tart, and nose-tinglingly spicy, as in well-seasoned. I inhaled it, sometimes in a small katori (bowl) but more often over a mound of perfectly cooked white rice. The fingers in my right hand, moving with the synchronized speed of a factory line worker, emptied the thali (platter) in no time, often skipping the buttermilk course in favor of a second helping of comforting rasam.

Rasam has often been called "molaghu tanni" ("pepper water"). When the first Englishman was served this thin broth, which is a southern Indian staple, he fell head over heels in love with it—but his clipped English tongue could not twirl the right way to enunciate the words. What came out sounded more like "mulligatawny" and the name stuck. It landed on the English table many reincarnations later, radically different from the original. It is undeniably *the* iconic soup that represents the quintessential Anglo-Indian food that spread to that spread throughout the British Empire. Lizzie Collingham, in her authoritative work *Curry: A Tale of Cooks and Conquerors*, shares the story of two sisters, Wilhelmina and Stephana Malcolm, in Dumfriesshire, Scotland, who corresponded regularly with their ten brothers living in India. The brothers sent their sisters recipes for mulligatawny and other Indian dishes, which they included in their kitchen notebooks. The British who lived in Madras (where the dish originated) soon garnered the nickname Mulls, as they couldn't conceive of the idea of a meal that would not start with their rendition of the soup, which now included rice, pieces of various meats, apples, chicken stock, and Madras curry powder. The British cook Mrs. Beeton had a version that included bacon, while poet and cookbook author Eliza Acton went in the surreal direction of incorporating pickled mangoes, calf's head, bull's testicle, and cream. Mercifully my version leaves those out!

Creamy Chicken Vegetable Soup with Apples

Mulligatawny ·•· Serves 8

2 tablespoons canola oil

2 pounds bone-in chicken thighs

1 medium red onion, finely chopped

1 medium green bell pepper, halved lengthwise, stemmed, seeded, and cut into ½-inch pieces

1 large carrot, peeled, finely chopped

1 large tart-sweet apple (like Honeycrisp, peeled, cored, and cut into ½-inch pieces

1 medium turnip, peeled and cut into ½-inch pieces

2 large stalks celery, cut into ½-inch pieces (including leaves)

4 large cloves garlic, finely chopped

2 large fresh or dried bay leaves

2 tablespoons Madras Curry Powder (page 19)

1½ teaspoons coarse sea salt

1 quart low-sodium chicken stock or broth

1 cup unsweetened coconut milk

1 cup frozen green peas (no need to thaw)

¼ cup finely chopped fresh cilantro

½ teaspoon black peppercorns, coarsely cracked

1 Heat the oil in a large saucepan or Dutch oven over medium-high heat. Once the oil appears to shimmer, carefully place the chicken pieces, skin side down, in the pan in a single layer. The oil will start to splatter (hence the "carefully" warning). Place a lid on the pan to contain the splattering. The meat will sear and turn reddish brown, about 4 minutes. Flip the pieces over and repeat with the other side, an additional 4 minutes. Lift the browned pieces of meat onto a plate.

2 Add the onion, bell pepper, carrot, apple, turnip, celery, garlic, and bay leaves to the oil in the pan. Cook the compote, uncovered, stirring occasionally, until partially tender, 7 to 9 minutes. Sprinkle in the curry powder and salt, giving it all a good stir or two. The heat is just right in the medley to cook the ground spices in the blend without burning them, about 15 seconds.

3 Nestle the chicken pieces back into the pan among the spiced fruit and vegetable medley, including any juices that pooled onto the plate where the chicken was temporarily stored. Pour in the stock and give it a stir or two. Bring the brothy curry to a boil. Lower the heat to medium and simmer vigorously, covered, stirring occasionally, until the chicken is cooked through (barely pink in the center and the juices run clear when pierced), 30 to 35 minutes.

(recipe continues)

4 Stir in the coconut milk and allow the curry to come to a boil again. Turn off the heat. Transfer the chicken into a bowl along with about two cups of the vegetables and fruit. If you have a stick blender, use it directly in the pan and puree the remaining mélange into a smooth and creamy blend. If not, a regular blender works great—you may have to do it in batches because of the large volume of the pan's contents.

5 If you used a blender, pour the pureed soup back into the pan. Stir in the peas. Keep it on low heat.

6 Add the reserved vegetables and fruit back to the soup. By now the chicken should be cool enough to handle. Tear the chicken meat from the bones and pile it on a cutting board. Cut it up into smaller pieces and add it back to the soup as well.

7 Discard the bay leaves. Sprinkle in the cilantro and black pepper and serve.

PLAYING WITH FIRE

The first curry house in London, Hindoostane Coffee House, opened in 1810. Although it didn't last long, it set the stage for the tsunami wave of curry houses that flooded the United Kingdom many decades later (in the 1970s), thanks to the influx of Indian and Bangladeshi immigrants. These restaurants served the foods that the Anglo-Indians in Britain craved—curries that had left a mark in their culinary memory. While most of these dishes were adapted to suit the Brits' relatively timid taste buds, fiery vindaloos (hotter versions were called tindaloos and bindaloos) always populated curry house menus, a tool for drunken revelers to show their prowess after a night of guzzling pints of pale ale.

The British, in their jostling with the Portuguese, Dutch, and French for control of Goa in southwestern India in 1797, were the first to "discover" vindaloo. The curry was in fact a Goan adaptation of a Portuguese dish called carne de vinha d'alhos: meat cooked in vinegar and garlic. (Incidentally, vinegar was not present in Goa when the Portuguese got there. They were only able to re-create this dish thanks to the ingenuity of some Franciscan priests, who figured out how to ferment coconut toddy.) The British managed to occupy Goa for 17 years before they relinquished it back to the Portuguese. But by then they had fallen in love with their Goan cooks, whose converted Christian beliefs freed them from the dietary mores that prohibited cooking beef and pork. Pork vindaloo became one of the Brits' favorite Anglo-Indian curries, and restaurateurs in the British curry houses (over 8,000 of them) upheld beguiling that love, using fresh spices instead of the Madras curry powder that had become so commonplace.

Fiery vindaloos work well with bowls of steeped white rice (see page 193) to absorb some of that potency. A side of yogurt will do the trick as well.

British Curry House Vindaloo

Pork vindaloo ·•· Serves 4

1 tablespoon coriander seeds

1 tablespoon cumin seeds

1 teaspoon black or yellow mustard seeds

1 teaspoon fenugreek seeds

½ teaspoon black peppercorns

Seeds from 2 or 3 black cardamom pods (see Note, page 116)

8 dried red cayenne chiles (like chile de arbol), stems discarded

2 sticks (about 3 inches each) cinnamon, broken into smaller pieces

1 teaspoon coarse sea salt

1 teaspoon sweet paprika or ground annatto (achiote) seeds

½ teaspoon ground turmeric

½ cup cider or malt vinegar

2 tablespoons mustard or canola oil

1 pound boneless pork loin chops, cut into 1-inch cubes

2 tablespoons finely chopped fresh ginger

8 medium cloves garlic, finely chopped

1 serrano chile, stem discarded, and cut into quarters lengthwise (do not remove the seeds)

2 tablespoons finely chopped fresh cilantro

1 Pile the coriander, cumin, mustard, and fenugreek seeds, peppercorns, cardamom seeds, cayenne chiles, and cinnamon into the bowl of a spice grinder (Or a clean coffee grinder). Grind the ingredients to the consistency of finely ground black pepper. Tap the lid to release any of the intoxicating blend back into the bowl's cavity. Dump this out into a small bowl and stir in the salt, paprika, and turmeric. Pour the vinegar over the spice blend and stir it in to fashion a thick slurry, slightly gritty and smelling potent-hot.

2 Heat the oil in a medium sauté pan over medium-high heat. Once the oil appears to shimmer, add the pork, ginger, garlic, and serrano chile. Allow the meat to sear, the ginger and garlic to lightly brown, and the chile to slightly blister, uncovered, stirring occasionally, 10 to 12 minutes.

3 Add the spice slurry to the pork and give it all a good stir. Lower the heat to medium. The vinegar in the paste will start to evaporate and the spices will start to cook, glistening the pan's contents with a light, oily glaze, 5 to 8 minutes. Be sure to keep the pan uncovered and stir occasionally to prevent anything from scorching.

4 Pour in ½ cup of water and scrape the pan to deglaze the pan drippings. Reduce the heat to medium-low and simmer the curry, covered, stirring occasionally, until the pork is tender, about 15 minutes.

5 Stir in the cilantro and serve.

FIT FOR A QUEEN

A formulaic, steadfast salad for sandwiches is this Anglo-Indian favorite called coronation chicken in the United Kingdom and curried chicken salad in the United States (quite popular in the 1960s and beyond). Its creation is attributed to Constance Spry (a florist and writer) and Rosemary Hume (the cofounder with Dione Lucas of l'École du Petit Cordon Bleu cooking school in London in the early 1930s) as part of the elaborate banquet during Queen Elizabeth II's coronation in 1953.

My version keeps it simple, layering the chicken with Madras curry powder as it cooks and also sautéing the spice blend with the other aromatics in the dressing. A common mistake many make is to add the curry powder directly to the dressing, which renders the dish chalky. If anything, learn to cook your spices without burning them. Raw, uncooked spices (with the exception of a few like cardamom and black peppercorns) are most unpleasant; when you soften the blend while cooking the base (the onion and chicken, in this recipe), the flavors are more nuanced.

Coronation Curried
Chicken Salad with Apricots

Serves 4

FOR THE CHICKEN

2 tablespoons canola oil

1 teaspoon Madras Curry Powder (page 19)

1 pound bone-in chicken breasts and/or thighs, skin removed (see Note)

½ teaspoon coarse sea salt

½ teaspoon coarsely ground black pepper

FOR THE DRESSING

2 tablespoons canola oil

1 small yellow onion, finely chopped

2 large cloves garlic, finely chopped

2 teaspoons Madras Curry Powder (page 19)

½ cup mayonnaise

¼ cup heavy (whipping) cream

¼ cup red wine

1 teaspoon Dijon mustard

2 tablespoons Major Grey's Mango Chutney, finely chopped (see Tips, page 169)

2 tablespoons finely chopped dried apricots

1 tablespoon freshly squeezed lime or lemon juice

1 teaspoon coarse sea salt

½ teaspoon coarsely cracked black pepper

1 To pan-roast the chicken, heat the oil in a medium skillet over medium-high heat. Quickly sprinkle and rub the curry powder on both sides of each chicken piece. Once the oil appears to shimmer, add the spiced chicken pieces, meat side down, and allow them to start searing. Sprinkle the top sides with half the salt and pepper. Let the undersides sear and turn light brown, 3 to 5 minutes. Flip the chicken pieces over and sprinkle with the remaining salt and pepper. Continue to cook until seared on the other side 3 to 5 minutes more.

2 Pour ½ cup water over the chicken pieces, scraping the bottom of the pan to deglaze it. Reduce the heat to medium-low and simmer the chicken, covered, flipping the pieces on occasion to ensure even cooking, until the pieces release a clear liquid when pierced in their thickest parts, 12 to 15 minutes. Transfer them to a plate and place in the refrigerator to cool (this can easily be made even a day ahead if you wish).

3 Meanwhile, make the dressing for the salad. Use the same pan you used to cook the chicken in, wiping it dry with a paper towel to remove any moisture that may make the oil splatter. Pour in the oil and heat it over medium heat. Once the oil appears to shimmer, add the onion and garlic and stir-fry the medley to take the edge off their pungency, 2 to 4 minutes. Sprinkle and stir in the curry powder; the heat will be just right to cook the spices in the blend without burning them, 15 to 20 seconds. Scrape the pan's contents into a medium bowl.

4 Add the mayonnaise, heavy cream, wine, mustard, chutney, apricots, lime juice, salt, and pepper and give it all a good whisk to fashion a dressing studded with fruit and infused with flavor.

5 Grab the cooled chicken out of the refrigerator and separate the meat from the bones (tearing it up into pieces by hand is the perfect way). Transfer to the bowl with the dressing along with any pooled juices from the plate. Give it all a good mix.

6 Serve the salad either chilled or at room temperature. It is also great spread in between good hearty slices of bread for sandwiches.

✦ *It is best to pan-fry (or roast) your chicken at home so you can customize the addition of spices and seasonings as the bird cooks. But using a purchased roasted chicken is also fine, as is using any leftover cooked chicken. Cooked turkey meat is also fair game instead of the chicken (a great thing to do when you've cooked a massive turkey for the holidays and are wondering what to do with the leftovers!).*

AN ODE TO THE VENETIANS

One of the most powerful civilizations in world history was the Roman empire, which lasted a thousand years. It began in the eighth century BCE and eventually controlled the North African coast, Egypt, southern Europe, most of Western Europe, the Balkans, Crimea, and much of the Middle East, including Anatolia, the Levant, and parts of Mesopotamia and Arabia. During this period, the southern coast of Egypt along the Red Sea dominated the pepper trade from India, siphoning the wealth from its trade toward greater control and power. By 200 CE, cuisines started to intermingle from Rome all across to northern China. Complex sauces emerged, incorporating techniques of fermentation, using starches as thickeners along with ground nuts and eggs, and adding condiments and spices to create nuanced flavors.

In 827 CE, the conquest of Sicily by Tunisia introduced the inhabitants not only to the religion of Islam but also to hard grain for pasta and to sugarcane. The Muslim era also brought pleasure gardens that, upon the Muslims' departure, were converted to kitchen gardens replete with vegetable plants and fruit trees. Other invaders like the Greeks, Arabs, Berbers, Moors, Cretans, Phoenicians, Carthaginians, and Normans brought in pecorino cheese (from sheep's milk), couscous, rice, and salted cod.

Venice's geographical position also made it a hub for trade and its cuisine a melting pot. Rice, gnocchi, raisins, breadcrumbs, and goose salami became the norm as did spices like cinnamon, cloves, peppercorns, and cardamom. The Jews in Venice made bigoli pasta with whole wheat and tossed it with anchovies and onions. Life after the Crusades in Venice saw the emergence of combinations like rice and peas, golden raisins (called sultanas—after the apocryphal story of a Turkish sultan who tossed away his white grapes while fleeing a tiger, those grapes drying into raisins in the blazing sun), and olive oil. Spices took center stage as the Arabs imported them into Venice. Soon pouches of spice blends scented many a Venetian dish—blends that included pepper, cinnamon, cloves, cumin, nutmeg, ginger, saffron, coriander, bay leaves, and more. In celebration of this port city's contributions to the spice trade, and the twisty role of whole wheat bigoli pasta, here is my homage to the Venetians.

Pasta with Pine Nut– and Raisin-Marinated Sardines

Bigoli con saor sarda ⦁ Serves 4

¼ cup distilled white, apple cider, or malt vinegar

2 tablespoons pine nuts, coarsely chopped

2 tablespoons golden raisins, finely chopped

1 can (about 4.25 ounces) boneless sardines (packed in oil or water), drained

1 teaspoon coarsely cracked black peppercorns

½ teaspoon whole cloves

½ teaspoon shaved nutmeg (see Tips)

¼ teaspoon saffron threads

1 tablespoon coarsely chopped fresh ginger

1 stick (about 3 inches) cinnamon, broken into smaller pieces

1 quart seafood stock (homemade or purchased)

1 pound dried or fresh bigoli pasta (see Tips)

1 cup plain or seasoned breadcrumbs, toasted (see Tips)

2 tablespoons extra virgin olive oil

1 Pour the vinegar into a small bowl and stir in the pine nuts and the raisins. Add the sardines to the sour-sweet marinade, making sure they are all well submerged in it. You can do this overnight or even just before you start prepping the stock and pasta.

2 Cut a 6-inch square of cheesecloth to use as a pouch for the spices. Place the peppercorns, cloves, nutmeg, saffron, ginger, and cinnamon in its center. Gather the edges to cover the spices and form a twisted bundle, also known as a spice sachet. Tie this up with string to securely contain the contents within.

3 Pour the stock into a medium saucepan and add the spice pouch to it. Bring it to a boil over medium-high heat. Once it boils, lower the heat to allow the stock to simmer

vigorously, uncovered, stirring gently and occasionally, to allow the stock to absorb some of the heady aromas and flavors from the pouch, 15 to 20 minutes.

4 Meanwhile, bring a large pot of water to a boil over medium-high heat for the pasta. Once the water comes to a rolling boil, add the pasta and cook it, uncovered, stirring occasionally, until the pasta is tender but firm. Allow 12 to 15 minutes if it's dried or 5 to 7 minutes if it's fresh.

5 Drain the pasta into a colander and give the colander a good shake or three to rid the noodles of excess water. Do not rinse them, as you want the starch in the pasta to allow the stock to evenly drape over the cooked noodles.

(recipe continues)

6 Transfer the noodles to a serving bowl; remove the spice sachet from the stock and discard it. Now pour the spice-perfumed stock over the pasta and toss well to evenly coat it.

7 Meanwhile, fish the sardines out of the vinegar marinade and chop them into bite-size pieces. Add the sweet-sour vinegar sauce to the pasta and give it another stir.

8 Serve the pasta topped with the sardines, the breadcrumbs, and a drizzle of olive oil.

TIPS

✦ You'll need cheesecloth and string to form a spice sachet.

✦ Marble-size whole nutmeg is easy to come by in the spice aisle of any grocery store. In fact, you should never buy preground nutmeg (or any spice if you can help it), as the freshly shaved or grated spice is superior in aroma and flavor. To shave a nutmeg, anchor a cutting board (by placing a damp paper towel or rubber mat underneath) and hold a nutmeg against it securely with the fingers of one hand. With the other hand, carefully run the blade of a sharp knife across the surface of the nutmeg. The resulting pieces will look a bit like pencil shavings.

✦ Bigoli (pronounced with a long "e" sound at the end) pasta, made from whole wheat flour, bears a resemblance to spaghetti in thickness, except the bigoli noodles are hollow inside. Specialty mail-order sources carry it, as do some stores that stock fresh pasta (yes, a simple Google search will reveal those resources). Buy either fresh or dried, but in case you can't secure bigoli, bucatini or spaghetti will work as a perfectly acceptable alternative.

✦ To toast breadcrumbs (which will intensify their nuttiness), preheat a skillet over medium heat. Once the pan is warm enough (holding your palm just above the base, you should feel heat within a few seconds), sprinkle the breadcrumbs into the pan and allow them to turn light brown, stirring the contents with great regularity, 3 to 5 minutes.

✦ Parmigiano-Reggiano is not a conventional sprinkle on pastas in this floating city, but don't let that prevent you from using it, since there are no bigoli pasta police hanging around your kitchen.

PONDICHERRY BY ANOTHER NAME

The French East India Company was the last of the European contingency to settle in India, in 1664, mostly in the southeast. Despite ongoing wars with the British armies during which control switched back and forth numerous times, France continued to hold on to a few cities in the southeast, Pondicherry being the most populous of them all. The French finally left the city formally in 1962, and the city's name was changed to Puducherry.

Located in the southeastern coastal area of India, Puducherry still retains the hallmarks of colonialism after more than 200 years, replete with influences of the English, Dutch, Portuguese, and French. It's the French legacy that continues to maintain a stronghold in the cuisine of this region, with homage to the baguette, croissant, pastry, and fresh-baked quiche. France too was beguiled by India's flavors, and upon return home, French expats incorporated many of India's spices and "curry" in their culinary repertoire. This factor, along with the presence of many communities from Morocco in France, resulted in the use of spice blends (like poudre de curry and ras al hanout) that added to the sophistication of French food. This fluffy egg quiche folds the flavor of curry into the pungency of Dijon mustard, tender spinach, salty olives, and nutty Gruyère cheese, all wrapped in a flaky, buttery, oh-so-French pie crust. Oui, c'est parfait!

Spinach and Olive Quiche with Ras al Hanout

Serves 6

FOR THE CRUST

1 cup unbleached white pastry flour, plus extra for dusting

½ teaspoon coarse sea salt

8 tablespoons (1 stick) butter, chilled

2 to 3 tablespoons ice water

FOR THE FILLING

1 tablespoon butter

½ cup finely chopped red onion

2 teaspoons ras al hanout (see page 106)

6 large eggs, beaten

1 cup heavy (whipping) cream

1 tablespoon Dijon mustard

½ teaspoon black peppercorns, coarsely cracked

½ teaspoon coarse sea salt

4 ounces fresh baby spinach leaves, finely chopped

½ cup sliced black olives

1 cup shredded Gruyère cheese

1 To make the crust, pour the flour and salt into a food processor bowl with the metal blade in place. Cut up the butter into large cubes and add it to the flour. Pulse the ingredients to break up the butter into smaller pellets as the flour coats them to fashion pea-size lumps.

2 Spoon the water through the feeding chute and continue to pulse the machine until the dough all comes together into a fairly cohesive ball. It may still be a bit loose. Empty the bowl's contents onto a clean board or counter. Gather the dough into a tight ball, compressing it. Do not knead it as you do not want to form a lot of gluten, which will make the crust chewy. Pat it down into a patty roughly 1 inch thick. The butter-marbled dough gives a clue to the crust's impending flakiness. Wrap it in plastic and refrigerate it as you make the filling.

3 Place an oven rack in the center of the oven and preheat the oven to 375°F.

4 To make the filling, heat the butter in a small skillet over medium heat. Add the onion and stir-fry until it is lightly brown around the edges, about 5 minutes. Sprinkle in the ras al hanout, giving it a good stir, the heat in the onion being just right to cook the spices in the blend without burning them, about 5 seconds. Set the skillet aside.

5 Whisk together the eggs and cream in a medium bowl. Mix in the mustard, pepper, and salt. Stir in the spiced onion.

6 Fold in the spinach, olives, and cheese and set aside as you partially prebake the pie crust.

7 Lightly flour a board or the countertop as you prepare to roll out the crust. Grab the chilled dough and roll it out to fit a standard deep-dish 9-inch pie pan with an extra inch for overhanging around the edge. Keep lightly dusting with flour (not too much) as needed to ensure a stick-free crust. Brush off any excess flour from both sides of the dough. Place it in the pie pan and flute the edges by lifting a piece of the rim of the dough all around and pinching it between your thumb and forefinger. An alternate tool is a fork: Press the tines of the fork into the dough around the edges of the pie plate's lip to create ridges.

8 Tear a piece of parchment paper that will cover the bottom and half of the sides of the pie pan. Cover the bottom with either marbles, baking stones, or dried beans to weigh the paper down. Blind bake (no, you don't have to cover your eyes; it's the name of the technique of prebaking) the crust in the oven until it is very light brown around the edges, about 15 minutes. Remove from the oven, then carefully remove the weights and the paper.

9 Pour the egg batter into the shell and return the pie to the oven to bake uncovered, until the center is set, 45 to 50 minutes.

10 Allow the quiche to cool a bit on a cooling rack before slicing.

FOR BETTER OR WURST

If a country has a museum dedicated to a particular dish (plus a musical and a book), it sheds light on the importance of that dish. Currywurst has satiated many a German and is considered the country's national snack, especially when chased with a few steins of dark beer. One school of thought places the creation of the spiced and saucy sausage in Hamburg in 1947, based on a novel, *The Invention of Curried Sausage* by Uwe Timm. The German Currywurst Museum Berlin recognizes Herta Heuwer as the creator of the concept: According to their records, she was a food stall owner who acquired ketchup and curry powder from a British soldier during the Allied occupation of West Berlin. As the story goes, she tossed those ingredients with pork sausage on September 4, 1949, creating a dish that was irresistible, affordable, and very filling—especially when accompanied by a pile of French fries and a dollop of mayonnaise. The combination became a favorite among the construction workers rebuilding the city, who needed plenty of fodder. Whatever its origins, currywurst is undeniably delicious. This is my version.

Sausages Smothered in a Spiced Ketchup

Currywurst ⋅•⋅ Serves 4

FOR THE SAUSAGES

1 tablespoon canola or olive oil

1 pound uncooked bratwurst or kielbasa

FOR THE SAUCE

2 tablespoons canola or olive oil

1 cup ½-inch pieces yellow onion

2 teaspoons Madras Curry Powder (page 19)

½ teaspoon coarse sea salt

½ teaspoon smoked paprika (see Note)

½ cup ketchup

1 tablespoon hot sauce (like Tabasco)

1 To cook the sausages, drizzle the oil in a medium skillet over medium heat. Once the oil appears to shimmer, add the sausages and allow them to sear. Cover the pan to contain the splattering and also to allow the meat to cook in the pent-up steam. Move the sausages around to allow for an even browning. Once they cook, and a thermometer when stuck in the thickest part of the sausage registers between 155°F and 160°F, 12 to 15 minutes, turn off the heat and let them sit covered as you get the sauce ready.

2 Heat the 2 tablespoons of oil in a small saucepan over medium heat. Once the oil appears to shimmer, add the onion and stir-fry until muddy brown around the edges and the center, 10 to 12 minutes.

3 Sprinkle and stir in the curry powder, salt, and paprika. The heat in the onion is just right to cook the ground spices without burning them, about 5 seconds.

4 Pour in the ketchup and the hot sauce. Reduce the heat to low and simmer the sauce, covered, stirring occasionally, until a glistening sheen appears on its surface (that's the essential oils being released from the spices), 10 to 12 minutes.

5 Scrape this mixture into a blender jar. Pour ¼ cup water into the saucepan and scrape the bottom to release any collected bits of spices and sauce. Pour this into the blender jar as well. Puree the sauce until smooth, scraping the insides of the jar as needed.

6 Transfer the cooked sausages to a cutting board and cut them into ½-inch-thick slices. Add them back to the skillet along with at least half of the sauce. Turn the heat back on under the skillet to warm up the meat and sauce.

7 Serve, passing the remaining sauce around in case anyone needs a bit more of that addictive spiced ketchup.

✦ *Smoked paprika, from Spain, is a result of pimiento peppers having been smoke-dried over oak. It is deep red and quite smoky, a distant cousin to sweet paprika. I feel its presence is subtle and essential in highlighting the sausage flavors as well acting as a haunting backdrop to the spices in the curry powder.*

TWO CULTURES, ONE DISH

Every foreign invasion and colonization of India had its deep influences felt in the years that followed, in everything from infrastructure to architecture to food. Portugal colonized the southwestern state of India called Goa by 1510, and remained there until 1961. In many ways, the Portuguese changed the culinary topography of the entire country by bringing in kidney beans, corn, tapioca, papayas, pineapples, guavas, okra, coffee, peanuts, peppers, potatoes, tomatoes, and many other fruits and vegetables from the New World.

I had the opportunity to visit Portugal in early 2020. I saw in museums ornate carriages that transported kings and queens, gilded coaches that bore gifts for the pope—both thanks to the explorer Vasco da Gama, who crossed oceans seeking the Indian spices that enriched the Portuguese empire. A lucrative spice trade was established that not only benefited Portugal's economy, but opened doors that enabled Jesuit missionaries to go to India seeking converts and allowed for the maintenance of a strong Portuguese foothold in Goa even after the departure of the colonial British. I knew that India's cuisine had benefited from the introduction of potatoes, tomatoes, and chiles (as mentioned above), but it seemed to me that the culinary stream hadn't flowed both ways. Here were two countries with a solid bond, both speaking the language of food, yet whose cuisines, it appeared, couldn't be further apart. I was mistaken.

One city that stuck with me on my travels was Sintra, a quintessential European town with rolling mountains and cobbled streets. Ambling down one of the steep streets, and after having sipped the local Ginga (a port) in a chocolate cup, I was drawn into a bakery. The display case offered the usual suspects—delectable pastries, puddings, and breads, plus some savories. What caught my attention was a triangular-shaped crispy pastry stuffed with curried cabbage. Upon inquiry with my broken Portuguese, the woman behind the counter said it was a chamuça. The uncanny resemblance to India's samosas didn't escape me, though the pastry shell was closer in texture to an egg roll skin. Perhaps India was not lost entirely on Portugal, as I started seeing chamuças everywhere in Portugal at other bakeries and in grocery stores.

Here is my version, spiced filling stuffed into phyllo sheets folded like flags and baked to get that perfect crunchy bite. And like the proverbial potato chip, you can't just have one!

Crispy Vegetable Curry Triangles

Chamuça ⋆ Makes about 16 triangles

2 tablespoons olive oil plus extra for brushing the phyllo

1 medium green bell pepper, stemmed, seeded, and finely chopped

½ cup thinly sliced scallion whites plus ½ cup thinly sliced scallion greens (keep them separate)

2 large cloves garlic, finely chopped

1 tablespoon shredded fresh ginger

2 cups finely chopped napa cabbage

2 tablespoons Madras Curry Powder (page 19)

1 teaspoon coarse sea salt

1 to 2 tablespoons piri piri sauce (see Note)

1 large carrot, peeled and shredded

½ cup finely chopped fresh cilantro

1 package frozen phyllo sheets, completely thawed

1 Heat the 2 tablespoons oil in a large skillet over medium-high heat. Once the oil appears to shimmer, add the bell pepper, scallion whites, garlic, and ginger. Stir-fry the medley until light brown around the edges, 2 to 4 minutes.

2 Pile in the cabbage and sprinkle in the curry powder and salt. Continue to cook the cabbage, uncovered, stirring occasionally, 2 to 4 minutes. You will notice a bit of dew on the cabbage's surface as a bit of the water gets released from its surface. This starts to release some of the browned bits of vegetables, effectively deglazing the pan.

3 Stir in the piri piri, carrot, scallion greens, and cilantro. If there is a lot of spice stuck to the pan, pour in ¼ cup water and scrape the bottom of the pan to get it all released and into the filling. Position a fine-mesh colander in a bowl and empty the skillet's contents into the colander. Allow any excess liquid to drain into the bowl, giving the filling a stir once in a while in the colander to facilitate that and to cool it.

4 Position an oven rack in the center of the oven. Preheat the oven to 375°F. Line a sheet pan with parchment paper. If you don't have parchment paper, lightly spray the pan with cooking spray.

5 Unfold the thawed phyllo sheets on the countertop. Have a clean and damp cloth on hand. Carefully peel a sheet of the phyllo from the pile and place it on a cutting board. Brush it with some oil. Repeat with three more sheets so you end up with a stack of four sheets. Be sure to re-cover the stack of unfolded sheets with the damp cloth every time you peel off a single sheet to keep them from drying out. With the longer side (it measures 13 x 9 inches) of the four-sheet stack facing you, cut the stack into four equal strips. Working quickly with one strip at a time, with the short edge facing you, spoon

(recipe continues)

a tablespoonful of the cabbage filling onto the center of that end of the strip closest to you. Here is where your flag-folding skills come in handy. Form a triangle by folding the lower left-hand corner of the phyllo up and over the filling to the opposite edge. Flip this triangle over itself, maintaining the triangular shape. Repeat these folds as needed until you get to the end of the strip. You should have a neat-looking triangle. If you have an uneven lip of phyllo at the end, brush that lip with oil and tuck it under. Repeat with the remaining three strips. You will need to repeat the four-sheet stack, strips, and triangles three times more to yield 16 phyllo triangles.

6 Arrange the triangles in a single layer on the sheet pan so there is a bit of space between them and brush the tops with a little oil. Bake on the center rack until they are sunny brown and appear flaky-crispy, 25 to 30 minutes.

7 Serve warm, as is, or with a dipping sauce of your choice.

✦ *Portuguese-African in its origin, piri piri sauce is made with the namesake chilies, a cultivar created by the Portuguese explorers in Mozambique when they colonized it in the 1500s. Barely an inch in length and red when mature and dried, these can pack a capsaicin level of 175,000 Scoville units. Often acidic with vinegar as its base, the sauce, or comparable varieties, populates the grocery aisles that stock ketchup and other sauces. If you can't find it, substitute a vinegar-based hot sauce such as Tabasco.*

A LOCAL EXOTIC

After 1947, when India gained its independence from Britain, a large number of mixed-race people immigrated to Australia—a continent that, under British rule, had had a long history of discriminatory immigration policies. Among these migrants were Indians as well as the descendants of Tamil and Sinhalese Sri Lankans who had married Dutch and Portuguese settlers and traders and who, after the Sri Lankan Civil War, were attracted to Australia's fertile lands (immigration was made easier after the formal abolition of its whites-only policy in 1973). This grand masala of immigrants created waves of change in the culinary world, and the British, with their early colonial influence from India, had already established in Australia a hunger for curry powders.

Frieda Moran, a scholar of Australian curries, hit it on the head. She said the developments of these British-influenced curry powders were a result of negotiations and collaborations between the Anglo-Indians (a self-identified term for white British people living in India) and the Indigenous Indians. In a Sydney newspaper in December 1813, a formal announcement of the importation of the blend known as curry powder clinched its important position in Australian kitchens. Curry pastes and various adaptations of curry powders flourished as further evidence of British appropriation of Indian food.

Various brands of curry powders vied for Australia's attention, including Vencatachellum (a Tamil name, an homage to *the* Madras-style curry powder) and Clive of India (Robert Clive having been the first governor of Bengal during the British Raj). Joseph Keen, a white British immigrant who had settled in Tasmania, concocted his curry blend in the early 1860s and appropriately labeled it Keen's Curry Powder, which grew to be Australia's most popular brand and was marketed as "made local with exotic India's flavors." With many reincarnations of spices used to fabricate the blend, the current formula includes celery seed and allspice and now resides with American spice sovereign McCormick & Company.

This iconic handheld scallop pie—a smaller version of the ubiquitous pot pie—marries a traditional English seafood studded roux "en croute" (in a pastry crust) with the flavor of Tasmania's very own Keen's Curry Powder. It's a prime (and delicious) example of culinary intersectionality.

Creamy Curried Scallop Pies

Makes 6 individual pies

4 tablespoons (½ stick) butter

1 pound shucked bay scallops (see Note)

1 medium shallot, finely chopped

1 large carrot, peeled, finely chopped

2 tablespoons unbleached all-purpose flour

2 teaspoons Keen's Curry Powder or Madras Curry Powder (page 19)

1 cup canned or boxed fish stock (or chicken broth)

½ teaspoon coarse sea salt

2 tablespoons crème fraîche or heavy (whipping) cream

Zest from 1 small lemon

2 tablespoons finely chopped fresh tarragon leaves

½ cup frozen green peas (no need to thaw)

Butter or cooking spray, for brushing muffin cups

1 large egg

1 tablespoon cool tap water

Flour, for dusting

3 sheets frozen puff pastry, thawed but chilled until use

1 Melt 2 tablespoons of the butter in a large skillet over medium-high heat. Once the butter foams, add the bay scallops and stir them around to coat completely, allowing them to warm up a bit, 1 to 2 minutes. Remove them onto a plate along with any residual liquid.

2 Wipe the skillet with a paper towel if it's too wet or cook off the excess moisture before you add the remaining butter. Once it melts, now over medium heat, add the shallot and the carrot. Stir-fry the medley to barely remove the pungency of the shallot, 1 to 2 minutes.

3 Sprinkle in the flour and continue to cook the ingredients to allow the flour to roast and turn ever so slightly brown, 1 to 2 minutes. Add the Keen's Curry Powder and stir it in, the heat in the roux just right to cook the spices without burning them, about 1 minute.

4 Pour in the fish stock, a little at a time, and whisk it in to make sure you have a lump-free broth. Add any pooled liquid from the scallops on the plate along with the salt, crème fraîche, and lemon zest. Simmer the sauce, uncovered, stirring occasionally, until the sauce thickens, 5 to 7 minutes.

5 Stir in the tarragon and the peas and turn off the heat. Allow the sauce to come to room temperature.

6 Prepare a six-cup muffin pan (the muffin cavity is roughly 3½ inches wide and 1½ inches deep) by lightly greasing the insides with either butter or cooking spray. Position a sheet pan on the oven's lowest rack and preheat the oven to 425°F.

7 Beat together the egg and cool water to create a wash for the pastry.

(recipe continues)

8 Lightly flour a board or counter and unfurl the tri-folded puff pastry sheets, bringing them almost to room temperature, but still slightly chilled, as it is easier to cut them when not so soft. With a 4-inch biscuit or cookie cutter, cut out four circles from each of the puff pastry dough sheets. You should have a total of twelve. Shove a dough circle into a muffin cup cavity, making sure the dough comes up along the sides. Divide the bay scallops into six portions, scooping each into the prepared cups. Spoon in enough of the herbaceous sauce to cover the scallops. Place the remaining circles on top, pressing the extra dough hanging along the sides with the top dough, making a well-covered pie. With a fork, crimp the edges to fashion a well-sealed pie.

9 Brush each top with the egg wash. Then, with a knife, slit each pie in the center, about ⅛ inch deep. Place the muffin pan on the sheet pan. Bake until the tops are a deep, sunny brown, 18 to 20 minutes. Remove the pan from the oven and let rest for 15 minutes. With a butter knife or a small spatula, remove the pies from the muffin pan and serve.

✦ *Marble-size bay scallops, part of the bivalve mollusk family, are sweet and delicate, and a bit pricier than the larger sea scallops. They usually come shucked (yes, you can shuck corn too!), and you can eat them raw (just like sweet corn off the cob) and marvel at their succulence. The shells are a cornucopia of pastel colors resembling unfurled Japanese fans. The first time I saw these shells used as decorative pieces at the table was at my dear friend and colleague Lynne Rossetto Kasper's (yes, that one!) dinner table housing delectable sea salts from across the globe.*

TIPS

✦ Serve the individual pies with a fresh green salad topped with tart-crisp apples and lightly dressed with a fresh tarragon vinaigrette.

✦ For an even better presentation, bake the pies in individual ramekins (same size as the muffin cups).

FIJI'S MELTING POT

The late 1880s saw an influx of Indians to Fiji, an island in the South Pacific, after the British had colonized it in 1874. Multiple waves of immigrants from the subcontinent arrived between 1879 and 1916 under Britain's indentured labor laws to work the sugarcane plantations. With people of Indian descent comprising about half of Fiji's population, the influence of Indian curries and curry powders is a given not only in its archipelago, but in other Pacific islands like Samoa and Tonga as well. Spice-heavy curries are more a reflection of the Indo-Fijians' southern Indian roots, a stark contrast to those with northern Indian backgrounds. Culinary assimilation was not easy to come by in Fiji as the immigrants hung on to their adopted potatoes, chilies, and tomatoes, produce that was not indigenous to India, but an introduction from the European traders via the New World. School lunches of dal and curry are now a steadfast presence all across Fiji, including its remote villages, with a heavy reliance on premade turmeric-heavy curry powders instead of homemade mixes.

Fijian curries incorporate ingredients and techniques from India, China, Melanesia, Polynesia, and Europe. Goat is one of the most accessible meats in the archipelago, and I have seen many different vegetables as part of this stew (taro, cassava, sweet potatoes, and greens). I do love the subtle flavors of amaranth greens in this version of mine, but feel free to use any vegetable of your liking, remembering that the cooking times may vary.

Goat Curry with Amaranth Greens

Serves 4

1 small red onion, coarsely chopped

4 medium cloves garlic

4 slices (each about the size of a quarter) fresh ginger

1 habanero chile, stem discarded

2 teaspoons Madras Curry Powder (page 19)

½ teaspoon fenugreek seeds

1 pound young goat meat or boneless lamb leg, sold as stew meat, cut into 1-inch cubes (see Tips)

2 tablespoons vegetable oil

1 teaspoon coarse sea salt

1 pound fresh red amaranth leaves, well rinsed, tough stems discarded (see Tips)

1 teaspoon garam masala (page 191)

2 tablespoons finely chopped fresh cilantro

1 Pour ½ cup water into a blender jar and pile in the onion, garlic, ginger, habanero, curry powder, and fenugreek seeds. Puree, scraping the inside of the jar as needed to fashion a fairly smooth paste redolent of the spices in the golden curry powder and the potency of the habanero chile.

2 Pour the spiced slurry over the goat and give it all a good mix to coat the meat. Refrigerate for an hour or even overnight for the flavors to permeate the meat.

3 Heat the oil in a medium saucepan over medium-high heat. Once the oil appears to shimmer, add the goat including all the spiced slurry that coats it along with the salt. Initially, the slurry will simmer and once the water in it starts to evaporate, the goat pieces will start to sear a bit as well. All this happens in the uncovered pan as you stir its contents occasionally, 12 to 15 minutes.

4 As the meat sears, this is your chance to get the amaranth leaves ready. Stack a dozen or so of the leaves on top of one another and cut them into thin, matchstick-like strips. Repeat with the remaining bunch.

5 Now grab handfuls of the leaves and stir them into the curry. Pour in 1 cup water and give it all a good mix. Once the liquid starts to boil, lower the heat to medium-low, cover the pan, stirring its contents occasionally, and cook until the meat is fork-tender and the greens, now olive green, are cooked as well, about an hour. Most of the liquid should be absorbed. If you leave the pot on higher heat, you will need to add a bit more water to make sure the curry doesn't burn.

6 Stir in the garam masala and serve sprinkled with the cilantro.

TIPS

✦ Kid goat, under six months of age, is the preferred choice for getting tender results much sooner. As the goat matures it gets tougher, and it takes much longer to cook (there is a reason why you call someone an old goat). Oftentimes, cooks prefer pressure cooking the meat for a quicker breakdown of its tough collagen. If you are comfortable making the curry in a pressure cooker, slow cooker, or an Instant Pot, by all means go ahead. Go to your city's African, Caribbean, or Latin American stores to procure fresh-cut goat meat. Lamb is a perfectly acceptable alternative, much more readily available, and is not as strong-tasting (as in gamy) as the goat.

✦ If you can't find amaranth greens at your market, or more likely, at an Asian grocery store, spinach, collard greens, mustard greens (slightly more bitter), and kale are all great stand-ins. Its name is derived from the Greek word for "unfading," and amaranth flowers produce a purple dye, which was deemed unsafe for humans in the late 1970s. Sometimes labeled as Chinese spinach, the leaves are mellow with a very slight bitterness. Used extensively in African, Indian, Caribbean, and Chinese cultures, amaranth is a nutritionally solid green with a high amount of protein. Its seeds in particular are considered a superfood because of that high protein content. I grew up on addictive puffed amaranth seed bars (which look similar to Rice Krispies bars sans marshmallows), and I still treat myself to them every chance I get.

4

THE
AMERICAS

The Age of Discovery also brought Europeans to a new group of continents, inhabited by many varied peoples, which we now call the Americas. And that fateful arrival also affected a gastronomical exchange. In so much of the world, curry means comfort—and that is especially the case in the Americas, where "curry" describes a range of rib-sticking dishes that speak loudly of home.

Italian explorer and colonizer Christopher Columbus, who famously mistook the islands of the Caribbean for the east coast of India, brought back to the Spanish monarch (his sponsor) what he identified as "pimenta," or pepper (i.e., black peppercorn). However, what he actually had in tow were two separate plants new to the European continent, a species of berry, which we now know to be called allspice, and chiles. In the fifteenth and sixteenth centuries, the Spanish colonizers brought French, West African, and Portuguese culinary influences (as well as their own, of course) to South America, the Caribbean, and Mexico. Later, in the eighteenth century, the United States made its first foray into spice trading from its Salem, Massachusetts, port.

Movement between these once isolated hemispheres established the opportunity to create foundational dishes of the treasured cuisines we still enjoy. The aromatic mélange that perfumes each dish is inflected not only by the people who make it, but also by local ingredients—in Mexico, spices, chiles, and cacao combine in rich, luxurious mole (essentially curry by another name); in the Caribbean, staple ingredients like goat and jackfruit become the toothsome foundation for stews abundant in spice and heat; and in the United States, curry powder, raisins, and a bit of homesickness for the British Raj gave rise to the South's traditional Country Captain chicken. Ever adaptable, curry takes nearly infinite—and always flavorful—forms.

CURRIED CHICKEN
with PEPPERS and RAISINS

Country captain chicken ✛

UNITED STATES

168

POACHED CHICKEN
with a SPICED MOLE SAUCE

Mole coloradito oaxaqueño ✛ MEXICO

171

BONE-IN GOAT
with HABANERO CHILE and POTATOES

Curry goat ✛ JAMAICA

177

FLATBREADS STUFFED
with CURRIED YELLOW SPLIT PEAS

Roti dal poori ✛ TRINIDAD AND TOBAGO

180

TRINIDAD and TOBAGO
CURRY POWDER

TRINIDAD AND TOBAGO

183

CURRIED CHICKPEA STEW SANDWICHES
with SCOTCH BONNET RELISH

Doubles ✛ TRINIDAD AND TOBAGO

185

CATFISH with
UNRIPE MANGO and THYME

Gilbaka curry ✛ GUYANA

190

AMERICA'S CAPTAIN

This curry holds iconic status among homes and restaurants in the southern United States, but let's not forget that its origins are deeply rooted in the Anglo-Indian community. Story has it that a country captain in the British Raj sailed to Charleston, South Carolina, and Savannah, Georgia, with spices from the motherland (the British named their trade ships "country ships," and the sea captains who manned them were thus dubbed "country captains"). Propelled by his hosts' warm hospitality, he showed them how to make a chicken curry and the resulting dish was aptly named Country Captain in his honor. More likely, the dish is the natural result of different cultures intermingling in the US South in the early nineteenth century.

The dish made its first printed appearance in Eliza Leslie's 1857 cookbook, *Miss Leslie's New Cookery Book*. A half century later, in Alessandro Filippini's 1906 cookbook, *The International Cook Book*, the recipe took on green peppers, garlic, and tomatoes, which brought it closer to my kind of ideal curry. However, it was chef Arie Mullins who popularized the dish by serving it to future president Franklin D. Roosevelt and General George Patton. (Mullins swapped canned tomatoes for fresh tomatoes.) The general was so smitten by the recipe that his cooks fed it to the American troops with some regularity.

Years on, Cecily Brownstone, a New York newspaper columnist for Associated Press, championed this curry and became the unofficial torch bearer of all things Country Captain (with help from James Beard). Cecily looked down on variations that did not meet her standards, expressing indignation when someone used chicken breast and cream in the recipe. "Using a breast, can you imagine?" she said in a telephone interview with cookbook author and columnist Molly O'Neill, "I don't want to give names—I really don't want to get into that—but can you imagine that someone actually used cream? Cream! And they called it 'Country Captain'! It is very discouraging."

I adapted this recipe from one created by my dear friends and colleagues Nathalie Dupree and Cynthia Graubart for James Beard award–winning cookbook *Mastering the Art of Southern Cooking* (2012). I've added some accoutrements, like golden raisins, coconut, and mango chutney, in keeping with the Anglo-Indian way of serving curries.

Curried Chicken
with Peppers and Raisins

Country captain chicken ⋅⇢⋅ Serves 4

1 whole chicken
(3½ to 4 pounds), cut
into 8 pieces (see Tips)

2 tablespoons butter

1 tablespoon canola oil

1 medium yellow onion,
finely chopped

1 large red bell pepper,
stemmed, seeded, and
finely chopped

2 large cloves garlic,
finely chopped

1 tablespoon Madras Curry
Powder (page 19)

¼ teaspoon ground red
pepper (cayenne)

1 can (28 ounces) diced
tomatoes, including juices

1 teaspoon coarse sea salt

½ teaspoon coarsely cracked
black peppercorns

½ cup golden raisins

½ cup blanched, sliced
almonds, toasted

2 tablespoons shredded
unsweetened coconut
(fresh or dried)

3 slices bacon, cooked
crisp, finely chopped or
crumbled

½ teaspoon dried thyme

¼ cup finely chopped fresh
flat-leaf (Italian) parsley

4 cups steeped Indian
or Pakistani white
basmati or jasmine rice
(see page 193)

¼ cup Major Grey's Mango
Chutney (see Tips)

1 Pat the chicken dry with paper towels to absorb the excess moisture.

2 Heat the butter and oil over medium heat in a large skillet or Dutch oven. Once it foams a bit and appears to shimmer, add the chicken, skin side down, dark pieces first, to the hottest part of the pan. Continue adding pieces in a clockwise fashion, to know which went in first, in a single layer without overlapping, and cook to a deep golden brown on the bottom, 5 to 7 minutes. Turn the chicken pieces with tongs, and brown on the other side, 3 to 5 minutes. Remove the chicken pieces onto a plate.

3 In the same pan, pile in the onion, bell pepper, and garlic. Stir-fry the medley to soften and render the vegetables slightly brown

around the edges, 3 to 5 minutes. Sprinkle in the curry powder and the ground red pepper, stirring them in. The heat will be just right to cook the spices without burning them, 5 to 10 seconds.

4 Pour in the tomatoes and their juices, stirring them around to release any collected bits of spices, vegetables, and chicken from the pan's bottom, effectively deglazing it. Return the chicken to the pan, skin side up, including any pooled juices on the plate; cover and simmer, stirring the pan's curry occasionally, flipping the chicken pieces as needed, until the chicken, when pierced in its thickest part, releases a clear liquid, about 30 minutes.

5 Lift the chicken pieces out of the pan onto a plate to cool. Once cool to the touch, separate the chicken meat from the bones and add the meat back to the sauce. Stir in the salt and pepper. Rewarm the chicken, uncovered, stirring occasionally over medium heat, about 3 minutes.

6 Serve the curry topped with the raisins, almonds, coconut, bacon, thyme, and parsley alongside the cooked rice and mango chutney.

TIPS

✦ You can procure cut-up chicken at your supermarket's meat counter. But a wealth of options open up if you get the whole chicken instead. Not only is it cheaper, the gizzards, liver, and other organ parts make great additions to the thrifty home chef's repertoire of dishes. To cut the chicken into 8 pieces, start at the legs. Clasp the legs together with one hand while slipping the other hand into the neck cavity for leverage. Wring the chicken as you would a wet towel, twisting will separate the top (breast and wings) from the bottom (legs). Separate the 2 legs and cut each leg in half at the joint, creating thigh and drumstick pieces. Place your thumb inside the neck cavity to find the base of the bone; pull hard to separate it from the cartilage. Cut the breasts apart by slicing each along the breastbone, then cut each breast in half crosswise to create four pieces, two with the wings intact. (If you prefer, you can separate the wings at the joint.)

✦ One school of thought places the creation of this mango chutney in the hands of Major Grey, a British army man stationed in India in the nineteenth century, but its roots can be traced to an iconic west Indian pickle called murabba (shredded unripe mango cooked under the sun's heat with cayenne, sugar, and cardamom). Mango chutney satisfies the Anglo-Indian taste for something both sweet and tart and perfectly compliments this dish. Thankfully, it can be found at most supermarkets these days.

CURRY BY ANOTHER NAME

I have always considered the regional cuisine of Mexico to be India's soulmate. Just take the world of chiles as an example. These fiery fruits native to Mexico proved to be an incredible find for India. Similarly, spices that were indigenous to India—such as black peppercorns, cinnamon, and cloves—are now commonplace in Mexico. Evidence of chiles in Mexico dates back as early as 7000 BCE; Indigenous peoples started cultivating them there in large quantities around 3500 BCE. And, of course, we know that in 1492, Christopher Columbus believed he'd anchored in India and discovered the pepper plant, when in fact he was at the opposite end of the world (the land now known as the Americas) and one of the plants he'd found was the chile (hence even today many call chiles "peppers" or just say chile peppers). In the early sixteenth century, the Portuguese took those chiles to India.

Mole, that most layered of sauces, weaves in those very same chiles plus herbs, spices, nuts, and chocolate. Sor Andrea de la Asunción, the head nun in the kitchen at the Santa Rosa convent in Puebla, Mexico, is credited with its creation. Synthesizing native ingredients with influences from Spain and the Islamic kitchen, as is shown by the inclusion of herbs, nuts, and aromatic spices, mole poblano (which uses native Mexican chile poblano) has remained Mexico's iconic dish since about the late seventeenth century.

This particular mole comes from my friend and colleague Susana Trilling, a chef, teacher, caterer, author (her book on the subject is titled *My Search for the Seventh Mole*), TV hostess, food consultant, and directora of Seasons of My Heart Cooking School and Sazón de Mi Corazón S.A. de C.V. (a purveyor of gourmet products from Mexico) in Oaxaca, Mexico. She and I have talked numerous times about Mexico's and India's culinary connection, which I dream of someday exploring in greater depth, and her mole reminds me of the layered techniques we employ in some regional Indian curries. I'll be the first to admit that this is a long recipe, but the detailed explanations help to maximize the flavors extracted from the ingredients and spices, all of which are easy to come by at any supermarket. Even though chicken and lard are part of the recipe, it is a cinch to swap those for vegan-friendly palates. Butter beans and similar heirloom varieties are good alternatives to chicken (I add 3 cups cooked beans when I'd normally add the chicken) and canola oil a good replacement for the lard. And be sure to use an unrefined sugar since refined sugar is not considered vegan.

Poached Chicken
with a Spiced Mole Sauce

Mole coloradito oaxaqueño ◆ Serves 6

FOR THE CHICKEN

1 large white onion, studded with 1 whole clove

2 medium to large celery ribs with leaves, or 1 celery heart with leaves

1 small head garlic, cloves separated and peeled

2 carrots, peeled and thickly sliced

1 sprig fresh thyme or ½ teaspoon dried thyme

1 dried or fresh bay leaf

1 whole dried red cayenne chile (like chile de arbol), stem removed

3 black peppercorns

1 whole allspice

1 whole (about 4 pounds) chicken, cut up into 8 pieces (see Tips, page 169)

2 teaspoons coarse sea salt

FOR THE MOLE SAUCE

1 small ripe (but firm) plantain or banana

10 medium to large dried ancho chiles, stems and seeds discarded (see Tips)

11 dried guajillo chiles, stems and seeds discarded (see Tips)

Boiling water, for rehydrating the chiles

2 black peppercorns

2 whole cloves

1 whole allspice

1 stick (about 1 inch) cinnamon

½ cup white sesame seeds

¼ cup lard or canola oil

½ small French baguette, cut into ½-inch cubes

1 tablespoon black or golden raisins

5 whole almonds (skin on)

1 small head garlic, cloves separated (skin on)

1 small white onion, quartered

1 pound ripe tomatoes, cored and quartered

¼ cup fresh oregano leaves or 1 teaspoon dried oregano

2 bars (totaling 6 ounces) Mexican chocolate (see Tips)

1 tablespoon white granulated sugar

2 teaspoons coarse sea salt

A stack of warm corn tortillas for serving

1 Pour 10 cups water into a large saucepan or stockpot. Add the onion, celery, garlic, carrots, thyme, bay leaf, cayenne chile, peppercorns, and allspice (all the ingredients for the chicken stock, except the chicken and salt). Bring to a boil over medium-high heat, then add the chicken pieces. Continue to simmer, now over low heat, uncovered, until the chicken pieces, when pierced with a fork or knife, release clear juices, about 1 hour.

2 Stir in the salt. Fish out the chicken pieces onto a plate. Strain the stock into a bowl large enough to accommodate it. Once cool, skim off any fat from the stock's surface.

3 As the stock simmers away, perhaps it's the best time to start on the mole. Bring 2 cups water to a rolling boil in a medium saucepan over medium-high heat. Preheat the oven to 350°F.

(recipe continues)

4 Wrap the plantain or banana in foil (skin on) and bake it in the oven until soft and mushy, about 30 minutes. Set it aside as you get the remaining ingredients ready.

5 Preheat a large, heavy-bottomed skillet (I love using a cast-iron pan for this) over medium-high heat. Toast the ancho chiles in the dry skillet, flipping them around as needed, until they acquire black spots on their skin and their aromas intensify, 5 to 8 minutes. Transfer them to a bowl.

6 Toast the guajillo chilies next in the same fashion, 4 to 6 minutes. Add them to the ancho chiles in the bowl. Pour the boiling water over the chiles to cover by a depth of 1 inch, and allow them to soften and reconstitute, flipping them occasionally to ensure a good soak, about 30 minutes.

7 In that same skillet, over medium-high heat, sprinkle in the peppercorns, cloves, allspice, and cinnamon. Allow the spices to toast and change color a bit, shaking the pan very occasionally, scenting the air with their heady aromas, 1 to 2 minutes. Transfer them to a medium bowl. Now sprinkle the sesame seeds into that hot pan, shaking the pan constantly to brown them, 30 seconds to 1 minute. Add them to the spices.

8 Heat 2 tablespoons of the lard in that skillet over medium heat. Once the fat appears to shimmer, add the bread cubes to it and toast them, stirring them occasionally, until they

QUIT EQUATING SPICE WITH HEAT!

There are numerous books on the world of chiles—whether spelled with an -e for New World varieties or with an -i for those used in Asian cuisines—and I can easily talk passionately for hours on the subject. But as far as I'm concerned, the primary gist is this: Each and every chile is different in shape, color, size, texture, aroma, and level of heat. Please don't equate heat with spice, as in "Ooh, is it spicy?" or even "I love spicy!" Spice to me refers to the world of spices; the majority of spices used in cooking are to impart aromas and flavors, not heat—that's a chile's job. Hot is a taste element; spicy is not. So to conflate spicy and hot does such a disservice to both. (Yes, I will step off my soap box for now, but know that at a moment's notice I can climb back on it.)

What generates heat in chiles is an oil called capsaicin (part of a group of capsaicinoid compounds). The thin white pith-like membrane that runs along a chilie's center houses this chemical. The level of capsaicin in each chile is measured in Scoville Heat Units (SHU), a system developed by a scientist by the name of Wilbur Scoville. Pure capsaicin measures around 15 to 16 million Scoville units (in terms of pain, kind of comparable to being bitten by a tarantula). The mildest chiles are bell peppers (at 0 SHU), while the hottest cultivar in the world—called the Carolina Reaper—clocks in around 2.2 million SHU. Drinking water when you eat something hot really doesn't do much to assuage the discomfort, but milk and other dairy products will tone that down, as will a hoppy beer.

are sunny brown and appear crispy, 12 to 15 minutes. Fish them out of the pan and add them to the toasted spices, leaving as much of the lard as possible in the pan.

9 Still working over medium heat, add the raisins and almonds to that remaining lard, stirring them very occasionally, and cook until the raisins swell up and the almonds turn nutty brown, 1 to 2 minutes. Add them to the spices-and-bread cubes medley.

10 Add the skin-on garlic cloves and onion pieces to that hot skillet (there should be enough fat coating the skillet), and cook, uncovered, stirring them occasionally, over medium heat until they soften and acquire a few brownish-black spots, 10 to 12 minutes. Once cool to the touch, separate the skin from the garlic cloves. Add this onion medley to the spice bowl.

11 In that same skillet, add the tomatoes and oregano and let them stew over medium heat, uncovered, stirring occasionally. Once the tomatoes release their juices, they will start to soften, reduce down, and get condensed, 15 to 18 minutes.

12 Now get a blender ready for lots of pureeing. Pour ½ cup of the chiles' soaking liquid into the blender jar. Then fish the chiles out of the remaining soaking liquid and add them to the blender. Puree them, scraping the inside of the jar as needed, for an even, smooth puree. If needed, add some more of the soaking liquid to get the blades running smoothly. Transfer the paste to a fine-mesh colander set over a bowl. Stir it so most of it goes down into the bowl.

13 Pour 1 cup of the chicken stock into the blender jar and add the baked plantain (remove the skin first and discard it) along with all the contents in your spice bowl. Puree it all, scraping the insides of the jar as needed, until silky smooth. Transfer this to a bowl.

14 Now add the reduced tomatoes to the blender jar and puree that as well. Scrape this into a separate bowl. Yes, I know: lots of pans and bowls. But that's what it takes!

15 Heat the remaining 2 tablespoons lard in a Dutch oven or large saucepan over medium-high heat. Once the fat appears to shimmer and is almost smoky, add the chile puree. Lower the heat to medium as it will start to splatter and bubble. Keep stirring it, very occasionally, uncovered, until the liquid reduces to a paste, 15 to 18 minutes.

(recipe continues)

16 Add the tomato puree to this and continue simmering vigorously, uncovered, stirring occasionally, to cook down, about 15 minutes. If need be, lower the heat a tad if it starts to bubble and spit. You want to make sure the mole does not catch on the bottom or start to burn.

17 Now add the spice puree and continue simmering some more, still uncovered, stirring occasionally, to allow it to thicken up and start bubbling, about 10 minutes.

18 Pour 4 cups of the stock into the pan and give it all a good stir. Once it comes to a boil, continue the brisk simmer, uncovered, stirring occasionally, until it is warmed through and the flavors have had a chance to mingle, about 20 minutes.

19 Now stir in the chocolate, a little at a time, stirring it in until it all melts. Then add the sugar and salt, giving it all a good mix.

20 Whatever stock you have left, bring to a boil in a medium saucepan. Add the chicken pieces to the stock and let them warm up, uncovered, 5 to 8 minutes.

21 Get the chicken pieces out of the stock and transfer them to a serving platter. Pour plenty of the mole sauce over the chicken and serve it warm with the corn tortillas on the side to mop up all that laborious goodness.

TIPS

✦ The two chiles used in this mole are quite mild in their heat levels. Anchos (around 2,000 SHU) are dried poblanos that have a chocolate-like undertone in flavor which makes them work wonderfully in moles. They're easy to procure at the supermarket. Guajillos (around 4,000 SHU) are a dehydrated variety of chile called mirasol (Spanish for "sunflower"). I have seen bags of guajillos in conventional supermarkets, but if you have access to a Mexican grocery store, you will definitely find them there.

✦ In addition to chiles, Mexico was home to wild cacao for 4,000 years. It was around 2,000 years back that the Maya domesticated it—chiles and chocolate, two gifts that keep on giving to the world. In her 1998 book titled *My Mexico*, the incomparable Diana Kennedy reminisces about the women who went to the markets to procure ground-up cacao fortified with almonds and sugar to make the bitter paste palatable for drinking and cooking. The British once found chocolate on a captured Spanish ship and they threw it overboard, thinking it was sheep's dung, but, once the world knew what deliciousness it had gained, it fell in love. Mexican chocolate tends to be a bit grainier and bitter and is often mixed with other ingredients like sugar, almonds, vanilla, cinnamon, and chiles. Any Hispanic market will stock this chocolate, or you can order it online. Alternatively, you can mix semisweet or bittersweet chocolate with the ingredients listed above to fashion a flavor profile similar to Mexican chocolate on your own.

JAMAICAN SOUL FOOD

You say "Jamaica" and, for some, visions of Bob Marley come to mind. The singer, songwriter, and pioneer of reggae music entered the world's mainstream riding a wave of peace and positivity. Jamaica also brought us the gift of its food. And, might I say, the island's contribution to the world of curry—most especially, curry goat—is just as powerful a symbol of Jamaica's good vibrations.

This dish's story has a sobering start, however. Trace the plate's timeline, from iconic dish to emergence, and you'll be brought to the island's first colonizers, the Spanish, as well as its legacy of enslaved and indentured workers later on by the British colonizers. From 1509–1655, Spanish colonizers ruled over the Caribbean island, where they virtually annihilated the Indigenous people known as the Tainos. The British assumed power next, for over 250 years, and, with them, brought enslaved Africans. Once slavery was abolished on January 1, 1808, indentured workers from China and India were gradually brought in to work the sugarcane plantations.

Between the remaining Indigenous population of Tainos, the remaining Spanish settlers, the English colonizers, the enslaved Africans, the Indian workers, and (later) the Jewish settlers, the vegetable, meat, fish, seafood, and fruit bowls of Jamaica brimmed with cassava, corn, sweet potatoes, callaloo, pimientos, chiles, crab, goats, plantains, sugarcane, pomegranates, grapes, beef, breadfruit, eggplant, sesame, okra, pigeon peas, and much more. With this, and even though Indians only made up 3 percent of the population, curries caught on like wildfire and fueled the creation of Jamaica's famous curry goat. They relied on commercial curry powders, but their versions incorporated the indigenous allspice. The notable curry goat is often reserved for special occasions like weddings—which might also include mannish water, a soup considered an aphrodisiac made with the goat's head, penis, and other parts meant to benefit the groom during his nuptial night. No, I don't have a recipe for that. Sorry! Scrumptious curry goat reflects Jamaica's layered history as well as its people's spirited palate, this is a must-try.

Bone-in Goat with Habanero Chile and Potatoes

Curry goat ·•· Serves 4

3 tablespoons canola oil

2 pounds cut-up (about 2-inch pieces), bone-in goat or lamb (see Tips)

1 medium yellow onion, finely chopped

4 medium cloves garlic, finely chopped

4 pieces (each about the size of a quarter) fresh ginger, finely chopped

1 habanero chile, stem discarded, finely chopped (do not discard the seeds)

2 teaspoons Madras Curry Powder (page 19)

1 teaspoon allspice, freshly ground (see Tips)

1½ teaspoons coarse sea salt

2 medium russet potatoes, peeled, cut into 2-inch cubes (see Tips)

1 tablespoon apple cider vinegar

2 tablespoons finely chopped fresh thyme

2 scallions, trimmed, white bulbs and green tops thinly sliced

1 Heat 1 tablespoon of the oil over medium-high heat in a Dutch oven or large saucepan. Once the oil appears to shimmer, add half the goat meat, making sure the pieces don't overlap. Allow the pieces to sear, uncovered, stirring them occasionally for an even browning, 5 to 8 minutes. Transfer them to a plate. Add another tablespoon of oil to the pan and repeat the browning with the other half of the goat meat, an additional 5 to 8 minutes. Add this batch to the first one that is resting on the plate.

2 Drizzle the last tablespoon of oil in the pan. Add the onion, garlic, and ginger and stir-fry the medley until light brown around the edges, 3 to 5 minutes.

3 Add the chile, curry powder, allspice, and salt. Give it all a good mix; the heat will be just right to cook the ground spices without burning them, 10 to 15 seconds.

4 Pour in 3 cups of water, scraping the bottom of the pan to release collected bits of browned meat, vegetables, and spices, effectively deglazing the pan to create that depth of flavors that defines a great curry.

5 Transfer the meat back to the pan along with any pooled liquid on the plate. Stir the contents well. Once the curry comes to a boil, cover the pan, reduce the heat to medium-low, and allow the meat to cook and start getting tender, stirring occasionally, about an hour. If the liquid is at a low level, stir in another ½ cup of water.

6 Add the potatoes to the curry and stir. Cover the pan again and continue to simmer, stirring occasionally, until the potatoes are cooked and the meat is very tender, 30 to 45 minutes.

7 Stir in the vinegar, thyme, and scallions and serve.

TIPS

✦ Your best chance of procuring bone-in goat meat is at a specialty store that stocks groceries from countries like India or Pakistan or the Caribbean islands. Butchers often stock bite-size bone-in pieces, which, thanks to the marrow, provide more succulence when cooked in a curry.

✦ Despite what its name may imply, allspice is not a blend of spices. It is in fact a single spice, the green berry of a tropical tree by the same name that, today, is cultivated primarily in Jamaica. It is often mistaken for peppercorn (pimenta, according to the Spanish traders) or cloves (because of the numbing oil, eugenol, which is present in both allspice and cloves). As with other spices, it is best to buy whole allspice berries (which turn reddish brown when dried) and grind them fresh when a recipe, such as this one, calls for it ground. A spice grinder (or a clean coffee grinder) does a great job of pulverizing them and releasing those heady aromatics contained within. Jamaicans use premade curry powders, but the main difference between those used in the rest of the world and the one in Jamaican curries is the inclusion of ground allspice.

✦ Keep the chopped potatoes submerged in a bowl of water. Drain and pat dry just before use.

EVERYMAN'S BREAD

You would be hard-pressed to find a country that doesn't have some kind of flatbread inextricably bonded to its cuisine. Every grain is cultivated, dried, ground into flour, mixed, formed, and baked with a seemingly primordial knowledge. The desire for its simplicity and deliciousness transcends caste, creed, and status. Among this hearty class of food is roti. In Indian kitchens around the world, roti is the generic term assigned to thin, pliable breads that wrap curries, stir fries, chutneys, and other such foods. In Trinidad and Tobago, however, this bread (which is made using the native unbleached all-purpose flour) has taken on newfound iconic status and represents the region as one of its most popular street foods. Best consumed fresh, steaming hot off the griddle, these soft and flavorful taste-bomb vehicles will blow you away.

Flatbreads Stuffed with Curried Yellow Split Peas

Roti dal poori ⋅⊷⋅ Makes 6 rotis

FOR THE FILLING

½ cup yellow split peas

1 teaspoon Trinidad and Tobago Curry Powder (page 183)

8 to 10 medium to large fresh curry leaves

1 Scotch bonnet or habanero chile, stem removed

¼ cup firmly packed fresh cilantro

½ teaspoon coarse sea salt

FOR THE DOUGH

3 cups unbleached all-purpose flour, plus extra for dusting

2 teaspoons baking powder

1 tablespoon demerara or granulated unrefined sugar

1 teaspoon coarse sea salt

Ghee (for homemade, see Variation, page 95) or canola oil for brushing

1 Start out by making the filling. Scatter the split peas into a small saucepan. Cover them with tap water and rinse them to clean and rid them of any dust or debris. Tilt the pan to drain the water. Repeat once or twice more. Then add 2 cups of water to the peas and bring them to a boil over medium-high heat. A layer of foam will rise to the top; skim this off and discard it.

2 Add the curry powder to the peas and give them a stir or two. Lower the heat to medium and continue to vigorously simmer the peas, uncovered, stirring occasionally, until the peas are tender (but not mushy), 25 to 30 minutes. Drain into a colander and transfer the peas to a sheet pan lined with paper towels (or parchment paper), spreading them out to dry.

3 Once they are dry to the touch, transfer the peas to a food processor bowl along with the curry leaves, chile, cilantro, and salt. Pulse the mélange to break down all the ingredients. You should end up with an almost powdery texture, slightly coarse, and speckled with the hues of the herbs and chile. Transfer this to a bowl while you make the dough.

4 Thoroughly combine the flour, baking powder, sugar, and salt in a large bowl.

5 Pour 1 cup of warm water over the flour mixture and quickly stir it in. The flour will still be very dry, with a few wet spots.

6 Pour a few more tablespoons of warm water over the flour, stirring it in as you go. Repeat until the flour comes together to form a soft ball; you will use about 1¼ or 1½ cups of warm water altogether. You want the dough to be very soft, close to being slightly sticky, so if you add an extra tablespoon or so, you won't hurt it. Using your hands (as long as they're clean, I think they're the best tool), gather the ball, picking up any dry flour in the bottom of the bowl, and knead it to form a smooth, soft ball of dough. If it's a little too sticky to handle, dust your hands with flour, but try not to add any more flour to the dough. Knead it for a minute or two. (If you used your hands to make the dough from the start, they will be caked with clumps of dough. Scrape them back into the bowl. Wash and dry your hands thoroughly and return to the dough to knead it. You will get a much better feel for the dough's consistency with dry hands.)

7 Cut the dough into six equal portions. Lightly grease a plate with ghee or oil. Shape one portion into a round, resembling a hamburger bun, about 2 inches in diameter, and place it on the plate. (To get a smooth round, cup the dough in the palm of your hand and use your fingers to fold and tuck the edges underneath; then rotate it, folding and tucking all around to get an evenly smooth ball.) Repeat with the remaining dough.

8 Brush the tops of the rounds with ghee, cover them with plastic wrap or a slightly dampened cloth, and let them sit at room temperature for about 30 minutes.

9 Lift a dough round onto a lightly floured surface and roll it out to about 3 inches in diameter. Place the semi-rolled dough in the palm of one hand. Place about 2 tablespoons of the filling on the circle's center. Lift and stretch an edge over the filling, rotating the dough in your palm as you close the loop. Seal and shut the twisted top and reshape it into a disc. Set it aside back on the plate to allow the gluten to relax again, about 10 minutes. Meanwhile, repeat with the remaining dough rounds and filling.

10 When ready to cook the stuffed rotis, preheat a large skillet (a griddle would be ideal) that is 12 to 15 inches in diameter over medium heat. Place a large piece of foil, folded in half, next to it on the counter, to stack the finished rotis.

11 While the skillet heats, grab a stuffed round and place it on a well-floured surface. I usually fill a sugar shaker (they usually have slightly larger holes) with unbleached all-purpose flour and use that to evenly coat the surface of the dough as I roll it out. You want a circle that is about 10 inches in diameter, evenly thin with no tears. Use as much flour as needed to roll it out. Brush off extra flour from the surfaces of the rolled dough.

12 Lightly brush the warm skillet with a coat of ghee or oil. Transfer the rolled dough to the skillet and allow it to cook until brown patches appear on the underside, 3 to 5 minutes. Brush the top side with ghee before you flip it over to cook that side as well, 3 to 5 minutes. Transfer this to the folded foil sheet to keep warm and supple as you continue cooking the rest, stacking them on top of one another when finished.

13 Serve while they are still warm.

> ## TIP
>
> ✦ These rotis will freeze well after they are cooked. To re-warm, thaw them at room temperature and cook them in a warmed skillet (do not microwave). An extra brush of ghee on both sides, after the roti is warm, livens it up.

THE CARIBBEAN QUEEN

Marla Kissoondath Singh Jadoonanan has opened and closed many chapters in her life. The expanse of her kindness, her credentials, and cooking acumen, though, have remained consistent and impressive. Born and raised in Trinidad and Tobago to immigrant Punjabi parents, she experienced the death of her mother at the tender age of eight. It was then, when her help was needed in the kitchen, that she began working with spice blends and pastes to make curries and breads. Spinach curries, legumes, rice, and (weekend treats) seafood and meat became the bridges that kept her family connected to its roots. Seven years after the death of her mother, her father also passed away. Marla emigrated to the United States to be with her older brother, Harry Singh (see page 184), in Minnesota. Here, she started life anew.

As she settled in, she helped Harry with his restaurant and studied to become a registered nurse. In her 20 years working as a nurse in emergency care, women's health, and hospice, not only did she maintain a zeal for feeding her colleagues the foods of her homeland, she also put in double duty helping her brother at his restaurant. She decided to open her own restaurant in Minneapolis in 2005 where she cooked and managed its operations until recently, when she closed its doors permanently. Her family's curry powder was her steadfast companion, as she roasted and ground spices with diligence to maintain the intrinsic flavors of her Trinidad and Tobago kitchen. It's a blend she still uses daily as she prepares meals for her family and, occasionally, for past clients (regulars at her restaurant) who get to experience the magic of sitting down at her table once more.

She maintains that here in the United States food is often taken for granted, as folks eat on the run. For Marla, cooking and eating are spiritual experiences, practices she never compromises. The spice blends and pastes that shore up her pantry become talismans, ways to conjure up not only an ancestry, but her own journey through life. Her next chapter is sure to be an exciting one.

Trinidad and Tobago Curry Powder

Makes about ½ cup

2 tablespoons coriander seeds

2 tablespoons cumin seeds

2 tablespoons bishop's weed seeds (see Note)

1 tablespoon fenugreek seeds

1 tablespoon mustard seeds

2 tablespoons ground turmeric

1 Preheat a small skillet over medium-high heat. Once the pan appears warm, add the coriander, cumin, bishop's weed, fenugreek, and mustard seeds; toast them, shaking the pan occasionally for an even toast, until the spices smell fragrant, the coriander and fenugreek seeds are reddish brown, and the airy-light bishop's weed jumps around a bit, 1 to 2 minutes. Immediately transfer the spices to a plate to cool. The longer they sit in the hot pan, the more burnt and bitter they will be. Once they are cool to the touch, place them in a spice grinder (or a clean coffee grinder) and pulverize them until they are the texture of finely ground black pepper. Tap the lid to release any of the intoxicating blend back into the grinder's cavity.

2 Transfer this into a small bowl and stir in the turmeric. Store in a glass jar with a tight-fitting lid in a cool spot outside the refrigerator.

➜ *For the unfamiliar, the name "bishop's weed" might suggest a similarity to a certain psychoactive plant. In fact, there's no relation. This wild-growing spice, indigenous to India, imparts a uniquely herbaceous flavor that enlivens many a curry. Also known as carom, ajwain, and ajowan, the seeds are light and almost celery seed–like in looks. Closer in taste and aroma to dried thyme (because of the essential oil they both contain, called thymol) with a peppery undertone, it is available in stores that sell Asian groceries and spices. Mail-order buying is definitely an option as well.*

HOMEMADE CURRY PASTE

Marla makes a paste to form the base of many of her curries. Here's her recipe for it. (Yield: ½ cup.) In a food processor bowl, combine 1 small yellow onion, coarsely chopped; ¼ cup firmly packed culantro (see Tips, page 191) or cilantro leaves and tender stems; 6 large cloves garlic; and 3 Scotch bonnet or habanero chiles, stems discarded. Puree the potent medley into a slightly chunky paste. Store it in a glass jar in the refrigerator, where it will last for almost two weeks. Freeze it for up to three months. A tablespoon or two, stir-fried in oil (do this in a well-ventilated space), will create the sauce for anything you want curried Caribbean style. A teaspoon or two of the curry powder is essential as well.

FROM HARRY, WITH LOVE

Arawak and Carib people made up the Indigenous populace in Trinidad and Tobago for 7,000 years before Christopher Columbus claimed the island cluster for the Spanish monarch in 1498. Spain ruled Trinidad and Tobago for the next 300 years, enslaving native people to work on sugarcane plantations. When the British assumed power in 1797, they replaced the Indigenous labor force, worked to death by the previous colonizers, with 20,000 enslaved Africans. And once slavery was abolished in 1833, more than 150,000 Indians migrated to Trinidad and Tobago from the northeastern and central parts of India on indentured servitude contracts. The migration created a powerful impact, enough that in the 1940s, travel writer Patrick Leigh Fermor observed that "wide tracts of Trinidad are now, for all visual purposes, Bengal."

Thus began the curry-fication (maybe not a word, but I think it should be!) of Trinidad and Tobago, where the migrant Indians-turned-locals transformed turned seafood, mangoes, okra, potatoes, callaloo (a member of the taro root family), tomatoes, poultry, beef, pork, goat, and lamb into curries that each defined individual home kitchens. Nobel- and Booker Prize–winning author V. S. Naipaul paints life in the Indian Trinidadian community in his novel *A House for Mr. Biswas*.

My exposure to curries from this country came via Harry Singh, a local restaurateur and second-generation Indo-Trinidadian in Minneapolis–St. Paul, who opened a Caribbean restaurant with his wife, Annmarie, in 1983. He migrated to Minneapolis–St. Paul and, with the help of iconic restaurant owner Al Nye (of Nye's Polonaise Room) and Hubert Humphrey (yes *that* one), he set down roots in this community. He loves the Scotch bonnet chiles of his childhood kitchen—when Singh says "hot," he means "fiery"—the average person (or even the adventurous capsaicin-lover) won't be able to eat more than a bite or two of his curries. I was especially intrigued with his dish simply called Doubles, a popular street food in Trinidad and Tobago, which he serves with a chickpea curry. I chickened out and only tried mild. Doubles consists of two perfectly fried balloons of all-purpose flour dough (similar to India's bhaturas and the fry bread of Indigenous Americans) sandwiching fresh cooked chickpeas mottled with his family's curry powder (see page 183). A dollop of his Scotch bonnet relish rounded the experience. I was hooked.

Curried Chickpea Stew Sandwiches with Scotch Bonnet Relish

Doubles ·•· **Serves 6**

FOR THE DOUGH

1 package (2¼ teaspoons) active dry yeast

2 teaspoons demerara or granulated unrefined sugar

1 teaspoon coarse sea salt

1 teaspoon Trinidad and Tobago Curry Powder (page 183)

¼ cup buttermilk (at room temperature)

2½ cups unbleached all-purpose flour, plus extra for dusting

Oil, for brushing the dough

FOR THE SCOTCH BONNET RELISH (MAKES ½ CUP)

1 medium red bell pepper, stemmed, seeded, and cut into 1-inch pieces

3 small to medium Scotch bonnet (or habanero) chiles, stems discarded

2 large cloves garlic (no need to peel)

½ cup firmly packed fresh cilantro

1 teaspoon coarse sea salt

FOR THE CHICKPEA STEW

3 tablespoons canola or olive oil, plus extra for brushing

1 small red onion, finely chopped

1 medium red bell pepper, stemmed, seeded, and finely chopped

2 large cloves garlic, finely chopped

1 tablespoon Trinidad and Tobago Curry Powder (page 183)

1 teaspoon coarse sea salt

2 cans (15.5 ounces each) chickpeas, including brine

FOR FRYING

Canola oil (see Tip)

---

1 Make the dough: Whisk together the yeast, ½ cup of warm water, sugar, salt, curry powder, and buttermilk in a small bowl to thoroughly dissolve the yeast.

2 Measure out the flour into the bowl of a food processor. With the machine running, pour in the yeasty, sunny-colored liquid via the chute. The dough should come together to fashion a ball. If still dry, pour in very warm tap water, a few tablespoons at a time, to make that happen. The dough should feel satiny soft, almost sticky, but not unmanageable. Transfer the dough onto a work surface (dusted with a little flour if necessary) and knead it to make it uniformly smooth, about 2 minutes. Brush the

dough with oil and place it in a medium bowl. Cover the bowl with either a damp dishcloth (clean, please!) or plastic wrap. Let the gluten rest and the dough rise to increase in size by about 70 percent, about 1 hour.

3 As the dough rises, make the Scotch bonnet relish. Preheat a medium to large, heavy-bottomed skillet (like a cast-iron or stainless-steel skillet) over medium heat. Once the pan is hot, add the bell pepper, Scotch bonnet chiles, and garlic. Toast the ingredients, stirring the contents occasionally, to allow for an even blister and roast, 12 to 15 minutes. Make sure you have adequate ventilation, as the chiles will send you into a

(recipe continues)

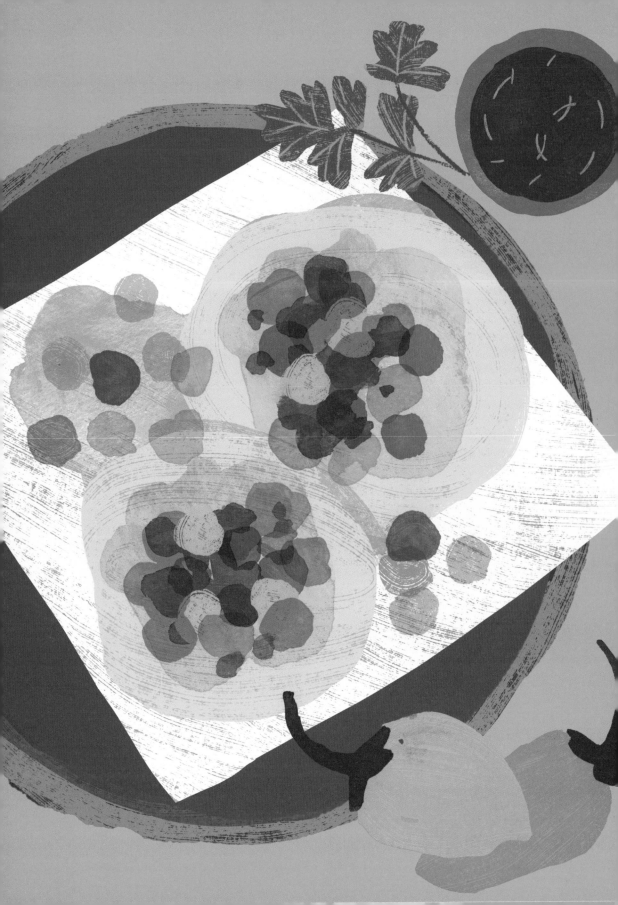

coughing fit. Cool them a bit so you can touch the garlic cloves to rid them of their skins. Transfer the medley to the food processor bowl and add the cilantro and salt. Pulse the mélange to an herbaceous and perfumed relish, slightly chunky and salsa-like. Transfer it into a jar or bowl and store it in the refrigerator, covered, until ready to serve.

4 Time to make the stew: Heat the oil in a Dutch oven or medium saucepan over medium heat. Once the oil appears to shimmer, pile in the onion, bell pepper, and garlic. Stir-fry the vegetables and let them initially sweat, then start turning light brown with a hint of rouge, about 10 minutes.

5 Sprinkle in the curry powder and salt, giving it a quick stir or two. The heat in the vegetables is just right for cooking the ground spices without burning them, 10 to 15 seconds. Pile in the chickpeas with their brine. Stir a few times to get it all incorporated. Bring the curry to a boil. Continue to vigorously simmer the curry, uncovered, stirring occasionally, until most of the liquid is absorbed into the beans, about 25 minutes. Turn off the burner and cover the pan to keep its contents warm as you fry the dough.

6 Now let's make the fried bread. Place a plate covered with paper towels near the stove to receive the finished breads. Pour oil to a depth of 2 to 3 inches into a wok, Dutch oven, or medium saucepan. Heat the oil over medium heat until a candy or deep-frying thermometer inserted into the oil (without touching the pan's bottom) registers 375°F to

400°F. (An alternative way to see if the oil is at the right temperature for deep-frying is to gently flick a drop of water over it. If the pearl-like drop skitters across the surface, the oil is ready. A safer way is to immerse a wooden skewer into the oil. Once bubbles surface from the skewer's pointed tip, the oil is ready.)

7 While the oil is heating, punch the dough down to deflate its ego. Divide the dough into 6 equal portions. Grab each portion and shape it into a round. Place the rounds on a plate to allow the gluten in them to soften up a bit (or your dough will spring back when you roll it out), about 5 minutes. Keep them covered with plastic wrap to prevent them from drying out.

8 When ready, lightly flour a small work area near the stove and place a dough patty on it. (Keep the remaining patties covered while you work on this one.) Roll it out to form a round, about 6 inches in diameter, dusting it with flour as needed. Make sure the round is evenly thin, with no tear on its surface. Repeat with the remaining rounds, stacking them as you make them, and flouring between the layers to prevent them from sticking to one another.

9 Once the oil is ready, slide a dough round into the pan. It will sink to the bottom, and then within seconds it will start to bubble and rise to the top. With the back of a spoon, gently keep submerging the round when it rises to the surface to enable the dough to puff from the inside. It will be done in less than a minute. Remove the sunny-brown bread with a slotted spoon and set it on the paper towels to drain.

(recipe continues)

TIP

→ Having been raised in a home where nothing was wasted, I find it downright sacrilegious not to reuse the oil that is left behind after deep-frying something. That said, the oil left after deep-frying meat is not suitable for a second fry because of the low smoking point produced by the water meat releases. Oil used with everything else (veggies, breads, and so on) will be okay. I usually filter the oil after use to rid it of any browned bits, store it in a glass jar, and refrigerate it. It can be reused once or twice more for deep-frying, but after that it is best used for stir-frying. Frugal? Yes. But not cheap!

10 Repeat with the remaining rounds.

11 To serve a double, grab a fried bread and slice it in half horizontally. Pile a generous portion of the chickpea stew on one half. Plop a dollop of the fiery Scotch bonnet relish (or two dollops if you are a hothead like me) atop the stew. Place the other half of the sliced bread on top and eat it like a sandwich.

GUYANA'S INDIA

Guyana, located on the northern coast of South America, gives every feeling of being a Caribbean island. It might owe that spirit to the fact that it's the only country in continental South America to have ever been under British rule (1831 to 1966), much like other Caribbean islands. (It was also colonized by the Dutch and French, prior to British rule.) The colony of Demerara, a historically important part of Guyana, plumb full of sugarcane plantations, is also the birth country of the widely used demerara sugar, a raw sugar not completely refined to rid the crystals of all molasses, giving the sugar its natural light brown shade.

Almost half of the country's population has roots in India. Britain's indentured labor system took Indian peasantry to Guyana under the promise of a "better life" including housing, medicine, food, and clothing, in exchange for minimal wages for five to seven years for back-breaking work. As a result, curries eventually made their way into every Guyanese kitchen. Seafood, mutton, and tropical fruits and vegetables were fair game for a curry—and the locally cultivated wiri wiri chiles brought the heat. Since these cherry-like chiles are harder to find in the United States, a Scotch bonnet or habanero chile will deliver an acceptably perfumed punch. Traditionally, this dish includes a scale-less variety of fish called gilbaker (pronounced gilbaka); very meaty and firm in texture, it is an unmatched delicacy in terms of a curry offering, especially when paired with the sourness of unripe mangoes, the scented allure of fresh thyme, and the heat from chiles. Just like those wiri wiri chilies, this fish is scarce in the United States, in fact it was banned by the US Department of Agriculture in 2018. Luckily, gilbaker is in the catfish family, making catfish the perfect substitute for this recipe!

Catfish with Unripe Mango and Thyme

Gilbaka curry ⋅⟶⋅ Serves 4

1 small yellow onion, coarsely chopped

2 large cloves garlic

2 teaspoons Madras Curry Powder (page 19)

½ teaspoon garam masala (for homemade, see Tips)

1 small habanero or Scotch bonnet chile, stem discarded

2 tablespoons canola oil

1½ pounds skinless catfish fillets

1 large unripe, stone-hard mango, peeled, and cut into ¼-inch cubes

1 teaspoon coarse sea salt

¼ cup finely chopped fresh thyme leaves (see Tips)

1 medium tomato, cored, finely chopped (no need to remove skin or seeds)

2 tablespoons finely chopped fresh culantro (see Tips) or cilantro

1 Plunk the onion, garlic, curry powder, garam masala, and habanero in a food processor's bowl. Mince the ingredients well. The perfume emanating from the bowl masks the searing heat from the habanero chile (if you wish you may discard its seeds before mincing, but Guyanese curries are all about heat).

2 Heat the oil in a large skillet over medium heat. Once the oil appears to shimmer, scrape the contents of the food processor's bowl into the hot oil. This is a great time to make sure you have your hood vent on high speed and perhaps open a window (or wear your handy pandemic mask). Stir-fry the pungent medley until the onion gets a bit translucent and the chile intensifies with its capsaicin aroma, 2 to 3 minutes. Place the catfish fillets atop the onion medley and let it absorb the flavors, 1 to 2 minutes. Flip the fish over and repeat with the other side, an additional 1 to 2 minutes. Remove the catfish onto a plate.

3 Add the mango to the skillet and give it all a good stir. Sprinkle in the salt, pour in ½ cup of water, and add the thyme. Scrape the skillet bottom to loosen up any browned bits of spices and fish. Return the fish, including any residual juices, to the skillet. Cover the pan and allow the fish to cook, spooning the mango and sauce over the fish periodically, until the fish barely starts to flake and the mango is fork-tender, 8 to 10 minutes.

4 Stir in the tomatoes and culantro, gently mixing the curry to get it all incorporated and to preserve the fish pieces in larger chunks as much as possible, and serve.

TIPS

✦ Garam masala is a combination of warming spices (garam is Hindi for "warm") that often includes cumin, coriander, cloves, cardamom, bay leaves, and peppercorns. The blends available for purchase are usually not toasted and so they will need to be added early on in the cooking so that they may lose their "rawness." With that, here's how to make your own in less than 5 minutes. In a small skillet, combine 1 tablespoon coriander seeds, 1 teaspoon cumin seeds, 1 dried bay leaf, ½ teaspoon black peppercorns, ¼ teaspoon whole cloves, the seeds of 4 green or white cardamom pods, and 2 dried red chiles (like chile de arbol), stems discarded. Toast over medium-high heat until they all darken a shade and smell fragrant, 1 to 2 minutes. Transfer to a plate to cool and then grind in a spice grinder (or a clean coffee grinder) to the texture of finely ground black pepper. Store in an airtight jar. It will keep for up to six months in a cool, dry spot in your pantry.

✦ Stripping the dainty leaves from fresh thyme stems is simpler than you may think. I hold the stem in one hand and run the fingers of my other hand in the opposite direction of growth. It's easy and perfumes my fingers in the bargain. It's alright if a few of the tender stems get added, but do be sure to pluck out any woody stems that get mixed in.

✦ Culantro, a pungent herb native to the Caribbean islands, is also known as false cilantro, spiny cilantro, or fitweed. Stronger-tasting than cilantro, it is sold in some stores that stock Southeast Asian, Caribbean, or Latin foods. By all means, use cilantro as an acceptable alternative.

MY STEEPED BASMATI RICE

Serves 6

It was that time of the week. The housekeeper had swept and mopped the floors around the home and then headed for the bathroom, where she soaked the soiled clothes in a red bucket filled with soapy water. She grabbed the baseball bat–like stick and thrashed the soaped fabrics with a rhythmic beat. Soon they made their way into a white plastic bucket filled with clean water for rinsing. Each piece of fabric was twisted dry, except for the cotton sarees that lay, beaten clean, in a twisted pile on the bathroom's white-tiled floor.

Meanwhile, my mother, Amma, was in the kitchen heating up a large stainless steel pot of water on a kerosene-fueled stove. She threw in a bowl of long-grain rice from a newer crop sold by the rice vendor who came to our door once a week with a large gunnysack trailing heavily over her left shoulder. The fresher the crop, the starchier the rice, I later found out, and this was important for Amma's impending chore. The water came to a second boil and the rice kernels rose to the top with each bubble, puffing up with the pride of having achieved destiny. The cooked grains clouded the water sticky white. With a slotted spoon Amma scooped out a few grains, squishing one between her thumb and forefinger to test its doneness. She was pleased to see it give in with no residual hardness. She placed a tight-fitting lid on the pot and lifted it off the stove. She placed the pot on its side, holding it by its lip with its lid slightly pulled back, at the sink's edge as a large bowl in the sink collected the starchy liquid. Sure, it would have been easier with a colander placed in a bowl, but she didn't have one of those.

She grabbed the starch-filled bowl and shuffled to the bathroom. She dunked the sarees, one at a time, coating each with the rice starch and letting it soak through. They rested fifteen minutes and then were lightly rinsed and wrung out by hand. Akka, my grandmother, awoke from her nap and grabbed the damp sarees that now lay in a bucket, waiting to be dried. She hung them out under the hot sun on the clotheslines pulled taut between two hooks nailed from each end of the balcony's wooden ledge. Once dry, the sarees were picked up by the ironing vendor. They came back into our home the same day, starched and neatly pressed, smelling like hot, steeped, nutty rice.

There are many ways to cook rice, especially one as refined as basmati. The two ideal ways are the absorption/steeping method and the open-pot pasta method. Some people use rice cookers and even pressure cookers to cook this delicate grain, but I find that they generate too intense a heat, resulting in a mushy, overcooked texture.

To salt or not to salt the rice? In my recipes for curries, stir-fries, and chutneys, I use just enough salt in the rice that accompanies them to bring out their flavors, so I do recommend salting the rice you'll be serving with them. If you don't salt the rice, you may want to add a bit more salt to the dish you are serving with it.

Absorption/Steeping Method

Makes 3 cups

1 cup Indian or Pakistani white basmati rice or jasmine or long-grain white rice

1 teaspoon coarse kosher or sea salt

1 Place the rice in a medium saucepan. Fill the pan with enough water to cover the rice. Gently rub the slender grains through your fingers, without breaking them, to wash off any dust or light foreign objects, like loose husks, which will float to the surface. The water will become cloudy. Drain this water. Repeat three or four times, until the water remains relatively clear; drain. Now add 1½ cups of cold tap water and let it sit at room temperature until the kernels soften, 20 to 30 minutes.

2 Stir in the salt and bring to a boil over medium-high heat. Cook, uncovered, until the water has been absorbed and craters are starting to appear in the surface of the rice, 5 to 8 minutes. Then, and only then, stir once to bring the partially cooked layer from the bottom of the pan to the surface. Cover the pan with a tight-fitting lid, reduce the heat to the lowest possible setting, and steep for 8 to 10 minutes (8 for an electric burner, 10 for a gas burner). Then turn off the heat and let stand, undisturbed, for 10 minutes.

3 Remove the lid, fluff the rice with a fork, and serve.

Open-Pot Pasta Method

Makes 3 cups

1 cup Indian or Pakistani white basmati rice or jasmine or long-grain white rice

1 teaspoon coarse kosher or sea salt

1 Fill a large saucepan halfway with water and bring it to a rolling boil over medium-high heat.

2 While the water is heating, place the rice in a medium saucepan. Fill the pan with enough water to cover the rice. Gently rub the slender grains through your fingers, without breaking them, to wash off any dust or light foreign objects, like loose husks, which will float to the surface. The water will become cloudy. Drain this water. Repeat three or four times, until the water remains relatively clear; drain.

3 Add the rice to the boiling water and stir once or twice. Bring the water to a boil again and continue to boil the rice vigorously, uncovered, stirring very rarely and only to test the kernels, until they are tender, 5 to 8 minutes. Immediately drain the rice in a colander and run cold water through it to stop the rice from continuing to cook. (The problem with this method is that the grain will go from just-right to overcooked in mere seconds if you are not attentive.)

4 Transfer the rice to a microwave-safe dish and stir in the salt. Just before you serve it, rewarm it in a microwave at full power, covered, 2 to 4 minutes.

CONVERSION TABLES

Approximate Equivalents

1 stick butter = 8 tbs = 4 oz = ½ cup = 115 g

1 cup all-purpose presifted flour = 4.7 oz

1 cup granulated sugar = 8 oz = 220 g

1 cup (firmly packed) brown sugar =
    6 oz = 220 g to 230 g

1 cup confectioners' sugar = 4½ oz = 115 g

1 cup honey or syrup = 12 oz

1 cup grated cheese = 4 oz

1 cup dried beans = 6 oz

1 large egg = about 2 oz or about 3 tbs

1 egg yolk = about 1 tbs

1 egg white = about 2 tbs

Please note that all conversions are approximate but close enough to be useful when converting from one system to another.

Weight Conversions

US/UK	METRIC	US/UK	METRIC
½ oz	15 g	7 oz	200 g
1 oz	30 g	8 oz	250 g
1½ oz	45 g	9 oz	275 g
2 oz	60 g	10 oz	300 g
2½ oz	75 g	11 oz	325 g
3 oz	90 g	12 oz	350 g
3½ oz	100 g	13 oz	375 g
4 oz	125 g	14 oz	400 g
5 oz	150 g	15 oz	450 g
6 oz	175 g	1 lb	500 g

Liquid Conversions

US	IMPERIAL	METRIC
2 tbs	1 fl oz	30 ml
3 tbs	1½ fl oz	45 ml
¼ cup	2 fl oz	60 ml
⅓ cup	2½ fl oz	75 ml
⅓ cup + 1 tbs	3 fl oz	90 ml
⅓ cup + 2 tbs	3½ fl oz	100 ml
½ cup	4 fl oz	125 ml
⅔ cup	5 fl oz	150 ml
¾ cup	6 fl oz	175 ml
¾ cup + 2 tbs	7 fl oz	200 ml
1 cup	8 fl oz	250 ml
1 cup + 2 tbs	9 fl oz	275 ml
1¼ cups	10 fl oz	300 ml
1⅓ cups	11 fl oz	325 ml
1½ cups	12 fl oz	350 ml
1⅔ cups	13 fl oz	375 ml
1¾ cups	14 fl oz	400 ml
1¾ cups + 2 tbs	15 fl oz	450 ml
2 cups (1 pint)	16 fl oz	500 ml
2½ cups	20 fl oz (1 pint)	600 ml
3¾ cups	1½ pints	900 ml
4 cups	1¾ pints	1 liter

Oven Temperatures

°F	GAS MARK	°C	°F	GAS MARK	°C
250	½	120	400	6	200
275	1	140	425	7	220
300	2	150	450	8	230
325	3	160	475	9	240
350	4	180	500	10	260
375	5	190			

Note: Reduce the temperature by 68°F (20°C) for fan-assisted ovens.

Abridged Bibliography

Achaya, K. T. *A Historical Dictionary of Indian Food.* Delhi: Oxford University Press, 1998.

——*Indian Food: A Historical Companion.* Delhi: Oxford University Press, 1994.

Anjum, Tanvir. "The Emergence of Muslim Rule in India: Some Historical Disconnects and Missing Links." *Islamic Studies* 46, no. 2 (2007): 217–40.

Appadurai, Arjun. "How to Make a National Cuisine: Cookbooks in Contemporary India." *Comparative Studies in Society and History* 30, no. 1 (1988): 3–24.

Buettner, Elizabeth. "'Going for an Indian': South Asian Restaurants and the Limits of Multiculturalism in Britain." In *Curried Cultures: Globalization, Food, and South Asia,* edited by Krishnendu Ray and Tulasi Srinivas. Berkeley: University of California Press, 2012.

Burton, David. *The Raj at Table.* Eastbourne, UK: Faber and Faber, 1993.

Collingham, Lizzie. *Curry: A Tale of Cooks and Conquerors.* New York: Oxford University Press, 2006.

Cramer, Marc. *Imperial Mongolian Cooking: Recipes from the Kingdoms of Genghis Khan.* New York: Hippocrene Books, 2001.

DeWitt, Dave. *Precious Cargo: How Foods from the Americas Changed the World.* Berkeley, CA: Counterpoint, 2014.

DeWitt, Dave, and Arthur J. Pais. *A World of Curries.* Boston: Little, Brown and Company, 1994.

Dupree, Nathalie, and Cynthia Graubart. *Mastering the Art of Southern Cooking.* Layton, Utah: Gibbs Smith, 2012.

Fernández-Armesto, Felipe. *Near a Thousand Tables: A History of Food.* New York: The Free Press, 2002.

Ferraro, Joanne M. *Venice: History of the Floating City.* New York: Cambridge University Press, 2012.

Freedman, Paul. *Out of the East: Spices and the Medieval Imagination.* New Haven, CT: Yale University Press, 2008.

Houston, Lynn Marie. *Food Culture in the Caribbean.* Westport, CT: Greenwood Press, 2005.

Hunt, Kathy. *Herring: A Global History.* London: Reaktion Books, 2017.

Ishige, Naomichi. *The History and Culture of Japanese Food.* London: Kegan Paul, 2001.

Laudan, Rachel. *Cuisine and Empire: Cooking in World History.* Berkeley: University of California Press, 2013.

Leong-Salobir, Cecilia. *Food Culture in Colonial Asia: A Taste of Empire.* London: Routledge, 2011. Taylor & Francis Group.

Lin, Florence. *Florence Lin's Complete Book of Chinese Noodles, Dumplings, and Breads.* New York: Quill, 1993.

Lovera, José Rafael. *Food Culture in South America.* Westport, CT: Greenwood Press, 2005.

Marks, Gil. *The World of Jewish Cooking.* New York: Simon & Schuster, 1996.

Moran, Frieda. "Ordinary and Exotic: A Cultural History of Curry in Australia." Bachelor's thesis, University of Tasmania, November 2017.

Newman, Yasmin. *7000 Islands: Cherished Recipes and Stories from the Philippines.* Hardie Grant, 2019.

Nguyen, Andrea. *Into the Vietnamese Kitchen: Treasured Foodways, Modern Flavors.* Berkeley, CA: Ten Speed Press, 2006

Nilsson, Magnus. *The Nordic Cookbook.* London: Phaidon, 2015.

Ono, Tadashi, and Harris Salat. *Japanese Soul Cooking.* Berkeley, CA: Ten Speed Press, 2013.

Ponseca, Nicole, and Miguel Trinidad. *I Am a Filipino: And This Is How We Cook.* New York: Artisan, 2018.

Reddy, Movindri. *Social Movements and the Indian Diaspora.* London: Routledge, 2015.

Regala-Angangco, Ofelia, and Adelisa Almario. "The Indian Community in the Philippines." *Philippine Sociological Review* 6, no. 2 (1958): 10–24. www.jstor.org/stable/43498034.

Rojanametin, Sarin, and Jean Thamthanakorn. *Bangkok Local: Cult Recipes from the Streets that Make the City.* Melbourne, Australia: Smith Street Books, 2019.

Schneider, Elizabeth. *Vegetables from Amaranth to Zucchini.* New York: HarperCollins, 2001.

Sen, Colleen Taylor. *Curry: A Global History.* London: Reaktion Books, 2009.

Sengupta, Jayanta. "India." *Food in Time and Place: The American Historical Association Companion to Food History.* Edited by Paul Freedman, Joyce E. Chaplin, and Ken Albala. Berkeley: University of California Press, 2014.

Singh, Dharam Jit. *Classic Cooking from India.* London: Arco, 1958.

Tan, Tony. *Hong Kong: Food City.* Sydney: Murdoch Books, 2019.

Thompson, David. *Thai Food/Arharn Thai.* Berkeley, CA: Ten Speed Press, 2002.

Middle Eastern & Islamic Cuisine; The Oldest Cookbooks in the World. Yale University Library Posters and Ephemera Concerning Events and Exhibits (RU 368). Manuscripts and Archives, Yale University Library, New Haven, CT.

Index